My Good Shepherd
Bible Story Book

Originally written by A. C. Mueller, D. D.
Artwork by Richard Hook

Selected and arranged by Lillian Brune

Concordia Publishing House
St. Louis

Concordia Publishing House, St. Louis, Missouri

Copyright 1969 Concordia Publishing House

Library of Congress Catalog Card No. 70-89876

9 10 11 12 13 14 15 16 17   KK   90 89 88 87 86 85 84

MANUFACTURED IN THE UNITED STATES OF AMERICA

Table of Contents

Adam and Eve in the Garden

Adam and Eve in the Garden

God planted a garden in Eden. He made many trees, which were nice to look at and were loaded with all kinds of fruit. A river ran through the garden. Gay flowers sprang up from the grass. Large and small animals played on the ground, the birds flew among the trees and filled the air with song. This beautiful place was more like a park than a garden, and we call it Paradise.

Here God put the man whom He had made. God called his name Adam. Paradise was to be man's earthly home. But he was not to live in idleness. He was to work and take care of the trees and the plants and the flowers.

In the center of Paradise stood a tree called the tree of life, and another tree, called the tree of knowledge of good and evil. The Lord God told Adam that he might eat of all the trees of the Garden except the second tree.

He said: "But of the tree of the knowledge of good and evil you shall not eat; for if you eat of it, you will surely die." God wanted to see whether Adam would obey His Word.

God also brought all the birds and the animals to Adam. He was to name them. But there was no creature that could talk to Adam and keep him company.

Then the Lord said: "It is not good for man to be alone; I will make him a helper." So God made the first woman, and He brought her to Adam, and she became his wife. Adam was very much pleased with her. He called her Eve.

Adam and Eve were very happy in their beautiful garden home. They were both made in the image of God and were good and without sin. God came to them and talked with them just as a father talks with his children.

They loved God. They also loved each other. Every day they thanked God for the many good things He had given them. Even caring for the garden was easy and pleasant because they loved God.

Genesis 2:1-23

Adam and Eve

How Sin Came into the World

Of all the creatures God made, the snake was the slyest. One day the devil, who tries to make all people do wrong, hid himself in a snake and came into the Garden of Eden.

He asked Eve: "Did God really say you should not eat of every tree in the garden?" Then Eve said: "We may eat of the fruit of all the trees. But of the fruit of the tree in the middle of the garden God said, 'You shall not eat of it, neither shall you touch it, or you will die.'"

But the snake said to Eve: "You will not die if you eat of that fruit; you will be as wise as God and know good and evil." Then Eve looked at the fruit of the tree and saw that it was good.

She ate of the fruit and gave some to Adam, and he also ate of it. But at once they found out that the devil had lied to them. They had disobeyed God. They had sinned. They felt ashamed and tried to hide.

When God asked Adam why he had eaten of the fruit, he blamed Eve. When God asked Eve why she had done this, she said, "The snake lied to me."

God had to punish Adam and Eve for their sin. He said they and all their children would have to die.

But God promised to send them a Savior. He cursed the snake and said that someday the Savior would come and would take away the devil's power. God meant that Jesus would come and die on the cross to save all people.

God told Adam that now he would have to work hard all his life and that at last he would die. He said that Eve, too, would have pain and sorrow and would die.

Then God drove them both out of the garden. He put an angel and a sword of fire at the gate, so that they could not come into the garden again.

That is how sin came into the world. Now everything was spoiled and no longer good, as it was when God made everything.

The devil brought sin into the world. When we sin, we are doing the work of the devil. Jesus is the only one who can save us and help us.

Genesis 3:1-24

Noah Coming Out of the Ark

The Flood

Adam and Eve had children, and their children had children. But all of them were sinful. After a long time there were many people on earth, and they were becoming more wicked than ever. When God saw this, He sent a great flood to punish them.

But one man feared God. His name was Noah. He and his wife had three sons. Each of their sons had a wife. So there were eight people in this family.

God told Noah to build a big ship, called the ark, because He was going to send the flood. There was to be room enough in the ark for Noah and his family and for some of all the different kinds of animals on earth.

Noah was also to tell the people that God would send a flood to drown them if they did not turn from their sins. God was patient and waited 120 years. But the people only laughed at Noah for building a ship on dry land. They did not turn from their sins.

At last the time for the great flood came. Into the ark Noah put food for the many animals and birds. God sent the animals and birds to Noah, and they went into the ark two by two.

Then Noah and his family went in, and God shut the door. Soon the rain began falling, and it rained for forty days and forty nights. Everything was covered with water. All the godless people and all creatures that live on land were drowned. But Noah and his family and the creatures in the ark were saved.

The flood lasted 150 days. Then God sent a wind to dry up the water. When the water went down, the ark landed on a mountain. After waiting a long time, Noah sent a raven and a dove from the window of the ark. The raven did not come back, but the dove came back with an olive leaf.

A week later Noah sent out the dove again, and it did not come back. So Noah and his sons took the cover off the ark, and God told them to come out. They had been in the ark a year and ten days.

Noah's family thanked God because He had saved their lives. Noah built an altar and gave an offering of thanks to God. God was pleased with the offering and promised Noah that He would never send such a flood again.

As a sign of this promise God set the rainbow in the sky. Every time we see a rainbow, it is to remind us of the great flood and of God's promise to Noah.

God saw that the hearts of the people were sinful even after the great flood. Yet He loved all men so much that many years later He sent His Son Jesus to take away the sins of the world.

Genesis 6:1 – 9:17

The Journey of Abraham

God Promises a Savior to Abraham

After the flood the human race kept on growing until there were many people on earth again. Most of them forgot God and began praying to idols.

In those days there was one man who believed in the true God and would not pray to idols. His name was Abram, and he had a wife named Sarai. Abram was a rich man. He had large flocks of sheep and herds of cattle and many servants.

One day God said to Abram: "Go away from your home to a land that I will show you. I will make of you a great nation, and in you all the families of the earth will be blessed."

This meant that God had chosen Abram and his family as the people among whom the Savior was to be born.

It was not easy for Abram to leave his home and all his relatives and friends. He had to travel far away with his flocks and herds.

He did not even know the name of the country where he was to go. But Abram loved God and willingly obeyed. He knew that God would watch over him on his journey.

He took his wife and servants and everything he had and went away. He also took his nephew Lot with him.

After a long journey Abram came to a country called Canaan, where there was much grass for his sheep and cattle. Here God spoke to him again, saying: "I will give this land to your children."

Abram lived in a tent and moved from one place to another. At each place he built an altar and prayed to God. He was thankful to God for leading him safely to this beautiful country.

Abram was seventy-five years old when he left home. It seemed strange to him that God had not given him any children. But the Lord came to him again and said: "Do not be afraid; I am your Keeper and your God."

When Abram complained that he had no children, the Lord took him out under the stars and said: "Look at the stars; that is how many children you will have."

When Abram was ninety-nine years old, the Lord said to him: "I am the almighty God; walk before Me, and obey Me." Once more God told him that he would have very many children.

God also changed his name from Abram to Abraham, which means "father of many"; and He changed Sarai's name to Sarah, which means "princess."

Although Abraham did not have even one child, he was sure God would keep His promise and give him many children. He also believed in the promised Savior and was happy to know that all his sins were forgiven.

Genesis 11:27-32; 12:1-9; 15:1-7; 17:1-8, 15-16

Servants of Abraham and Lot Quarrel over the Best Land

Abraham and Lot

God blessed Abraham in the land of Canaan. He let him become very rich in sheep and cattle, gold and silver. Abraham's nephew Lot also had flocks and herds and servants.

Both men needed plenty of grass and water for their sheep and cattle. Before long their servants began to quarrel over the land where the grass was best and over the wells of water.

When Abraham heard about this, he said to Lot: "Let us not have any fighting, for we are brothers. You leave me. If you want to go to the left, I will go to the right; if you want to go to the right, I will go to the left."

Abraham was older than Lot, and God had given him the land of Canaan. He might have chosen first. But Abraham was kind and let Lot choose the land he wanted. He was a peacemaker.

Lot was not unselfish like his uncle. He looked about; and when he saw the rich land near the Jordan River, he chose this good land for himself.

Now Abraham had to move away to another place where he could find grass and water for his flocks. But God came to Abraham again and promised to give the whole land of Canaan to him and his children.

Lot had chosen the best land for himself, but his choice was not a wise one. Two cities were there, Sodom and Gomorrah. The people in these cities were very wicked.

First Lot set up his tent near Sodom; then he moved into the city. Some time after he had made his home in Sodom, four kings came from other countries and carried off Lot and his family and all his goods.

Now Abraham showed again that he was kind and unselfish. He gathered his servants together and risked his life for Lot.

He came upon the kings and their soldiers during the night and drove them away. He saved Lot and brought him back with his family and all his goods.

Genesis 13:1-18; 14:8-16

Abraham and His Young Son, Isaac

God Gives Abraham a Son

Abraham was resting under a tree outside of his tent, for it was noon, and the sun was hot. As he looked up, he saw three men coming, and he ran to meet them. He made a deep bow and invited them to his home.

He said: "I will send for some water for you to wash your feet. Stay with us, and rest, and have something to eat before you go farther." They were willing to be his guests; so Abraham ran into the tent and told Sarah to bake some cakes.

He sent a servant to get a calf ready for the table. Sarah had butter and cheese, too. While the men were eating, Abraham stood near them to serve the food. One of the men was the Lord, the other two were angels.

After they had eaten, they asked: "Where is Sarah?" "She is in the tent," said Abraham. "Next year, when I come back," said the Lord, "Sarah will have a son."

Now, Sarah was listening, and when she heard this, she laughed. "Abraham and I are too old to have children," she thought.

The Lord said to Abraham: "Why did Sarah laugh?"

Sarah became afraid and denied it, saying: "I did not laugh!" But the Lord said: "Sarah, you did laugh."

After that the Lord and the two angels started to walk toward Sodom, and Abraham went with them a little way. Because Abraham was a friend of God, the Lord told him what He was going to do. He said He would destroy wicked Sodom.

At once Abraham thought of Lot, who lived there, and Abraham prayed to God. He wanted to save Lot. Later the Lord burned Sodom with fire from heaven, but He first sent the angels to lead Lot out of the city.

Before another year passed, a son was born to Abraham and Sarah. At last God had kept His promise as Abraham always believed He would.

The parents named him Isaac, which means "laughter," and watched happily as he grew up to be a fine young man.

Genesis 18:1 – 19:25; 21:1-8

Jacob Receives His Father's Blessing

Jacob Receives His Father's Blessing

Abraham and Sarah were very happy when their only son, Isaac, married a godly and beautiful woman named Rebekah.

God gave Isaac and Rebekah two sons. They were twins, and their names were Jacob and Esau. Esau, the first-born, had coarse and hairy skin. He liked to go hunting but cared very little about God's Word. Jacob loved God's Word and took care of the sheep and cattle.

Isaac loved Esau more, but Rebekah loved Jacob more. Even before they were born, God said the older brother should serve the younger.

When Isaac was old and almost blind, he said to Esau: "Go and kill a deer, and prepare the kind of meal I like, and I will bless you before I die."

Rebekah heard what Isaac said. She had Jacob kill two goats, and she made a good meal for Isaac. She dressed Jacob in Esau's clothes, covered his smooth skin with goatskin, and told him to take the meal to Isaac. Jacob lied to his father, saying he was Esau.

After Isaac had eaten, he gave Jacob the blessing. Esau cried when he found that Jacob had received the blessing. He hated Jacob and said he was going to kill him.

Now Rebekah called Jacob and told him to go to her old home and stay there until Esau's anger was over. Jacob said good-bye to his parents and started out alone.

When night came, he slept outside along the road. One evening, when it grew dark, he put some stones together for a pillow and lay down and had a wonderful dream. Jacob dreamed that he saw a ladder standing on the ground and reaching up to heaven.

The angels were going up and coming down, and God was at the top. God said: "I am the God of Abraham and Isaac. In you all the families of the earth will be blessed. I am with you and will keep you safe." In these words God gave Jacob the promise of the Savior.

When Jacob awoke, he said: "This is the house of God and the gate of heaven." He set up a stone to mark the place and poured oil on it. He called the place Bethel, which means "house of God."

Jacob promised to serve God all his life and to give back to God one tenth of all the things which God would give him. He went on, happy to know that God had forgiven his wrongs and would be with him.

Genesis 24:51-67; 25:21-28; 27:1 – 28:22

Reconciliation of Jacob and Esau

Jacob's Return to Canaan

After Jacob had that wonderful dream, he went on until he came to the land where his mother's relatives lived. He went to his uncle, whose name was Laban. He stayed with his uncle twenty years.

Laban had two daughters, Leah and Rachel. Jacob worked for Laban, seven years for each daughter. They became the wives of Jacob. Then Jacob worked for Laban six more years.

God blessed Jacob and made him very rich. God also gave Jacob twelve sons and a daughter. The twelfth son, Benjamin, was born later in Canaan.

At last God told Jacob to go back to the land of Canaan. It was a long and slow journey, for they had to drive all the great flocks and herds belonging to Jacob.

When they came near to the land of Canaan, Jacob remembered how angry Esau had been with him. So he sent messengers to Esau with a friendly message.

But the messengers came back to Jacob and told him that Esau was coming with four hundred men. Jacob was afraid that Esau would destroy him and his family and take all his goods.

Jacob had no soldiers to fight for him, but he prayed to God. He prayed that God would save him from his brother Esau. He said: "I am not worthy of the least of all the mercies and of all the truth which Thou hast showed unto Thy servant." Jacob knew that all the things which he owned had been given him by God.

That night Jacob was alone at the river. A man came to him in the night and began to wrestle with him. This man was God. Jacob knew that he could not win by his own strength, but he would not give up the fight.

He said to the Man: "I will not let Thee go except Thou bless me." Then God blessed Jacob again and said: "Thy name shall be called no more Jacob but Israel, for as a prince hast thou power with God and men."

Then Jacob went to meet Esau and his soldiers. But Esau did not fight with Jacob. Jacob bowed himself to the ground before his brother. Esau ran to meet him, put his arms around him, and kissed him. They both cried for joy.

Then Esau went to his home, and Jacob now lived in the land of Canaan. So God kept His promise and blessed Jacob. God keeps all His promises to us.

Genesis 29:1 – 33:20

Joseph's Dream

Joseph Sold by His Brothers

Jacob and his family now lived in the land of Canaan, which God had promised to Abraham, Isaac, and Jacob. Joseph, the second youngest of Jacob's sons, was God-fearing and obedient.

Jacob loved him more than all his other children, and he made him a coat of many colors. When his brothers saw this, they hated Joseph and would not speak a kind word to him.

Once Joseph had a dream, and he told it to his brothers. He dreamed that he and his brothers were in the field binding sheaves of grain. Joseph's sheaf stood up straight, and all the sheaves of his brothers bowed down to his. The brothers hated Joseph for this dream.

Another time he dreamed that the sun, the moon, and eleven stars bowed to him. When he told this dream, even his father scolded him. "Shall I and your mother and your brothers bow down to you?" he asked. Because of these dreams Joseph's brothers were jealous of him.

Later the brothers of Joseph were away from home a long time with their flocks and herds. "Go to your brothers," said Jacob to Joseph, "and see whether it is well with them and with the flocks." Joseph obeyed his father and went to look for his brothers.

When his brothers saw him coming, they said: "Here comes the dreamer. Let us kill him, and we shall see what will become of his dreams." But the oldest brother, Reuben, said: "Let us not kill him. Let us put him into this empty well."

Reuben wanted to come back later and pull Joseph out of the well and send him back to his father. When Joseph came up to them, the brothers took his coat of many colors away and put him into the empty well. Then they sat down to eat.

While they were eating, they saw some merchants passing by. One of his brothers, Judah, said: "Let us sell Joseph to these merchants."

So the brothers lifted Joseph out of the empty well and sold him to the merchants for twenty pieces of silver. The merchants took him far away to Egypt. There they sold him as a slave.

The wicked brothers took Joseph's coat and dipped it in the blood of a goat and showed it to their father. Jacob knew the coat and thought that a wild animal had killed Joseph. Jacob cried and cried for his dear son.

But God was with Joseph, and many years later both dreams of Joseph came true.

Genesis 37:1-36

Joseph Interprets Pharaoh's Dreams

Joseph in Egypt

Joseph was sold as a slave. An officer of the king of Egypt bought him. Even as a slave Joseph was faithful in all his work. His master put him over his whole house, because he saw that God was with Joseph. But his master's wife was a wicked woman and wanted Joseph to make love to her. Joseph would not listen to her.

He said: "How can I do this great wickedness and sin against God?" Then he ran out of the house. That night this bad woman told lies about Joseph, and his master became very angry and put him into prison.

But God was with Joseph even in prison. Soon the keeper of the prison put Joseph over all the prisoners, because he saw that he could trust him.

Sometime after this, two servants of the king were thrown into prison. The one was the king's butler, who made wine for the king. The other was the king's baker, who baked bread for the king.

One night both of these men had strange dreams. When Joseph saw that they were sad, he asked: "Why are you so sad today?" They answered: "We had a dream, and there is no one to tell us its meaning." Joseph said: "Tell me your dreams; maybe God will show me what they mean."

The butler told his dream, and Joseph gave the meaning. "After three days the king will forgive you and put you back in your old place," he said. Joseph asked the butler to remember him and tell the king about him.

The baker also told his dream, and Joseph gave the meaning. "After three days the king will hang you," he said. Both dreams came true just as Joseph had said. But the butler forgot Joseph. Joseph had to stay in prison two more years.

Then Pharaoh, king of Egypt, had a strange dream. He dreamed that he was standing by the river. He saw seven fat cows coming out of the river. Right after them came seven thin cows and ate up the fat cows. Later that night the king had another dream. He saw a stalk of wheat growing with seven full ears on it. Right after that he saw a stalk with seven empty ears, which ate up the full ears.

In the morning Pharaoh called all his wise men to find out what the dreams meant. But none of them could tell him. At last the butler remembered Joseph and told Pharaoh that Joseph could explain dreams.

"Bring Joseph to me," said the king. When Joseph came, the king asked him whether he could explain dreams. "I am not able of myself to do it," said Joseph. "But God will give Pharaoh an answer."

God showed Joseph the meaning of the dreams, so that he could tell it to Pharaoh. He said that both dreams meant the same thing. There would come seven years of great plenty. After that would come seven years of famine, when the people would not have enough to eat.

Joseph told Pharaoh to gather the great crops of the seven rich years into storehouses and to save this food for the seven poor years.

Pharaoh was much pleased with Joseph and told him that he should be the second ruler in the kingdom and should gather the food in the seven rich years.

He said Joseph should ride in his second-best carriage, and he put his own ring on Joseph's finger and put a fine gold chain about his neck. Then Joseph drove through the city and the land, and everywhere the people bowed before him as the second ruler of Egypt.

Genesis 39:1 – 41:43   23

Joseph Forgives His Brothers

The Journeys of Joseph's Brothers

After seven years of plenty the famine came. All the people had to go to Joseph to buy food. Jacob, the father of Joseph, lived in Canaan with his family.

When he heard that there was food in Egypt, he sent ten of his sons to buy food. Benjamin, his youngest son, he kept at home.

When the brothers came to Egypt, Joseph knew them at once; but they did not know him, for it was twenty years since they had sold him. When they bowed before him, Joseph remembered his dreams.

He also remembered how unkindly they had treated him, and he wanted to find out whether they were still so wicked. He spoke roughly, saying: "You are spies." They denied this, saying: "We are all sons of one man, and the youngest is with our father." "You must prove whether you are speaking the truth," said Joseph. "Unless you bring your youngest brother, you will be treated as spies."

Joseph put them in prison three days. Then he kept one brother, Simeon, in prison and sent the other brothers home to get Benjamin. Joseph told his servant to put each one's money into his sack.

On the way home the brothers found their money in their sacks and were still more afraid. They told their father everything. He said he would not let them take Benjamin to Egypt. But finally he had to let Benjamin go along because they again needed food.

This time Joseph brought them into his house and gave them a feast. When Joseph saw Benjamin, he had to go into another room to keep them from seeing him cry.

At the table he placed them according to their age. He also sent five times as much food to Benjamin as to the others. He wanted to see whether they were jealous of their brother. He also told his servant to put their money into their sacks again and to put his silver cup into Benjamin's sack. Then he sent them away.

They had not gone far when Joseph's servant ran after them and said: "One of you has stolen my master's silver cup. The one with whom the cup is found shall be my slave." They opened all the sacks and found the cup in Benjamin's sack. At once they all went back and begged Joseph to let Benjamin go.

Now Joseph could not keep his secret any longer. He told the other people to go out of the room. Then he said to his brothers: "I am Joseph."

He cried for joy and fell on Benjamin's neck, and Benjamin cried on his neck. At first the brothers were afraid; but Joseph kissed them all and told them to go to their father and tell him the good news and bring him to Egypt.

The king of Egypt even sent wagons to get Jacob and all his goods, and promised to give him a new home in Egypt.

Genesis 41:53 – 45:28

Finding the Baby Moses

The Birth and Flight of Moses

After Joseph died, the Children of Israel lived in Egypt many years. Another king ruled, and he did not remember all the good Joseph had done for Egypt.

When the new king saw that the Children of Israel were growing in number, he was afraid they would take his country from him. So he made them work like slaves. They had to bake bricks for his big buildings. But this hard work only made them stronger and greater.

Then this wicked king made a cruel law. He said that every baby boy who would be born to the Children of Israel should be thrown into the river. He thought there would be fewer and fewer people if no more men would be growing up.

In those days one woman of Israel had a sweet baby boy. She did not want to have him thrown into the river, so she hid him for three months. But when he began to cry and she could not hide him any more, she made a basket and put the baby into the basket. She took the basket to the river and said to Miriam, the baby's sister: "You stay here, and watch the basket."

After a little while the daughter of the king came with her maids to bathe in the river. They saw the basket. One of the maids brought it to the princess. They opened the basket and saw the baby boy. He was crying.

The princess pitied the poor baby and wished to bring him up as her own son. "Shall I go and get a woman to nurse the child for you?" asked Miriam, who had been hiding near her brother. "Yes," said the princess.

Miriam ran home and brought her own mother to the princess. The princess said: "Take this child and nurse it for me, and I will pay you." How glad they were to keep their baby boy!

When the boy grew up, the princess took him into the palace. She called him Moses, which means "Taken from the water." She sent him to school, and he learned many things there. But Moses knew he was one of the Children of Israel and not an Egyptian.

One day Moses went out to a place where some of his own people were working as slaves. He saw a man of Egypt beating a workman of Israel. This made Moses angry.

He thought no one was looking, so he killed the man of Egypt and buried him in the sand. But the king heard of this and wanted to kill Moses. So Moses ran away to the land of Midian.

Exodus 1:1 — 2:15

Crossing the Red Sea

Crossing the Red Sea

When Moses was eighty years old, God sent him back to Egypt to lead the Children of Israel away from slavery. But the king said: "I do not know your God; neither will I let the people go."

Then God sent lice, and flies, and sickness, and hail, and locusts, and other punishments upon the people of Egypt.

Each time God sent a trouble, the king promised to let the people go; but as soon as the trouble was over, he would not keep his promise. The last and worst punishment was that God let the first-born son in every Egyptian family die.

Then there was great weeping and sadness all over the land of Egypt, and the king said the people could go.

The Children of Israel hurried away from the land where they had worked as slaves. There were hundreds of thousands of men, women, and children, and they took with them all their cattle and everything they had.

God was with His people. He led them by day in a pillar of a cloud and by night in a pillar of fire. Soon after they were gone, the king and his men were sorry they had lost so many slaves.

Once more the king tried to fight against God and began to chase after the Children of Israel. His horsemen could go much faster then the people of Israel, who had to walk and had children and old people with them.

Before long the king and his soldiers caught up with them. The people of Israel were near the Red Sea. They were very much afraid. They knew they could not fight against the soldiers, and they feared they would all be killed.

But Moses said: "Fear not; stand still, and see how the Lord saves His people." Then the Angel of the Lord, who had led them, moved behind them and came between the Children of Israel and their enemies.

God told Moses to stretch out his hand over the sea, and God made a dry road for His people right through the Red Sea. The water stood up like a wall on each side, and the people walked through on dry land.

The king and his soldiers ran into the sea after them. But before they caught up with the Children of Israel, Moses stretched out his hand once more, and God made the waters come together again.

The king and all his soldiers were drowned. That is how God showed His power over the wicked king and saved His people.

Now Moses and all the Children of Israel sang a song of thanks to God. They sang: "The Lord is my Strength and my Song, and He has become our Redeemer. The horse and his rider He has thrown into the sea."

Exodus 3:1 — 15:21

Finding Manna in the Desert

Israel in the Wilderness

After the Children of Israel had crossed the Red Sea, God led them through a wild and dry country, called the wilderness. There was very little to eat in the wilderness, and sometimes water was scarce.

But God cared for His people in a wonderful way. After they had traveled three days, they came to Marah. The word "Marah" means bitter. The water at this place was so bitter that the people could not drink it.

They complained to Moses. Moses took this trouble to God in prayer. The Lord then showed Moses a tree. The Lord said: "Throw some of the branches of this tree into the water." Moses did this and the water at once became sweet, and everyone could drink all he wanted.

The Children of Israel had brought some food with them out of Egypt. But there were so many mouths to feed that this did not last long.

Soon the people began to say that Moses had led them out of Egypt only to let them die in the wilderness. They said they were sorry they had ever left Egypt.

Yet God was very good to them. He told Moses that He would send them both bread and meat. And He kept His promise in a very wonderful way.

In the evening God sent large flocks of birds called quails to the camp of Israel. There were so many that the people could easily catch them. Soon they had the finest meat, for quails are very good to eat.

Early the next morning God sent Israel the bread which He had promised. When the people rose from their sleep, the ground was covered with little round pieces of food. It tasted like cookies made with honey.

The Children of Israel called it manna. It was bread from heaven. For forty years, while they were on the way to the Promised Land, the Children of Israel ate this manna.

Now the people were satisfied for a while. But as they traveled, they came to a place where there was no water. God told Moses to strike a certain rock with his rod.

Moses did this and a stream of water flowed from the rock, and all the people could drink. That is how the heavenly Father cared for His people in the wilderness.

Exodus 15:22 — 17:6

Moses Receives the Law

The Giving of the Law

God wanted the Children of Israel to be His people. He promised that He would always be with them if they would obey His will. He told them what they were to do to show that they were His people.

When the Children of Israel had traveled about three months, they came to Mount Sinai. Here God was going to give the Ten Commandments to His people.

He said Moses should tell the people to wash their clothes and be ready for the third day. No one was to touch the mountain; so Moses built a fence around it.

At the sound of the trumpet on the third day, all the people were to come near the mountain.

In the morning of the third day all the people heard the trumpet. There was thunder and lightning, and a thick cloud was on the mountain. The people were afraid. When they came near, God said: "I am the Lord, thy God."

When all the people saw the lightning and the mountain smoking and heard the thunder and the noise of the trumpet, they ran back and stood afar off. They said to Moses: "You speak to us, and we will listen; but let not God speak to us lest we die."

Moses now went into the cloud on the mountain where God was, and God gave Moses two flat pieces of stone with the Ten Commandments written on them.

Exodus 19:1 – 20:21; 31:18

Going to Worship in the Tabernacle

The Tabernacle

God had given the Ten Commandments to Israel. But they also needed a place of worship. So Moses went up into Mount Sinai again. There the Lord told him that the people should make a holy place for Him because He wished to live among them.

He gave Moses the exact pattern of the holy place. The people lived in tent homes, and God's house was to be something like that. It was to be a tent church, called the Tabernacle, which could be taken down and set up again.

When Moses came down from the mountain, he called the people together for a meeting. He told them of God's plan and said: "Whoever is willing may bring an offering for God's house."

The people went home and willingly brought their gold jewelry. They gave silver also, and brass and wood and linen and skins of animals. Some of the women who knew how to spin made yarn and gave it to Moses. The people offered more than was needed.

Some of the men were skilled in weaving and in working with gold and silver. They had charge of the work and taught others.

These wise men and their helpers made golden vessels for the church and hammered some of the gold out in thin sheets.

They made boards and posts and covered them with gold. They wove cloth and made curtains and veils, or cloth hangings, for the Tabernacle.

They made a table and an altar and a candlestick of gold. They made an altar of brass and a large basin, or tank, to hold water for washing.

The finest thing they made was the Ark of God. It was a wooden box, or chest, covered with gold on the inside and outside. The lid was of gold, and on each end of the lid stood an angel made of gold. Into this Ark Moses put the two stone tables with the Ten Commandments.

When the work was finished, Moses set up the boards and spread four curtains over them, to form a tent.

This church was divided into two rooms by a costly veil. The Ark of God was put in the one room, which was called the Holy of Holies. The golden altar, the table of showbread, and the candlestick were put in the other room, which was called the Holy Place.

Around the tent was a yard, called the court. Pillars were set up around it, and curtains were put on them. But a doorway was left open for the priests to enter. In the court stood the altar of burnt offerings and the tank of water.

When everything was ready, Moses burnt incense on the golden altar and offered sacrifices on the altar of burnt offerings. A cloud also came down and rested on the tent church. The cloud showed that the Lord was there. So everyone knew that the Lord had come to live among His people.

Exodus 25:1 – 31:11; 35:4 – 40:38

Moses Looking at the Promised Land

Moses' Farewell and Death

The Children of Israel had come to the Jordan River. On the other side was the Promised Land, the country God had promised to Abraham and his people.

But God decided not to let Moses enter the Promised Land because at one time he had disobeyed God. God said to Moses: "Go to the top of the mountain and see the land which I have given to the Children of Israel. Then you will die."

Moses loved the people and wanted them to keep on serving God. If they had no good leader, they would become like sheep without a shepherd and would wander away from God. That is why he prayed to the Lord and asked Him to choose another man to take his place.

Joshua was a man who loved and trusted God very much. He had also helped Moses rule the people. So the Lord said to Moses: "Take Joshua and lay your hand on him and put him before the congregation so that all the people will obey him."

Moses did as God told him. He made Joshua the new leader of the people whom they were to honor and obey.

Then Moses had a farewell meeting with his people. For the last time he reminded them of God's commandments and of all that God had done for them.

He summed up God's law in the words: "Thou shalt love the Lord, thy God, with all thy heart and with all thy soul and with all thy might." He also told the fathers to keep God's words in their hearts and to teach them daily to their children.

Moses promised the people God's blessing if they would keep God's commandments. He told them that they would be happy in their homes and in their work and that the Lord would bless everything they did if they would love and obey Him.

But if they did not obey the Lord, God would punish them, Moses warned. When Moses had finished speaking, he raised his hands and gave the Children of Israel a farewell blessing.

After this, Moses went up into the mountain, and God showed him the Promised Land with its beautiful hills and rich fields and valleys. There on the mountain Moses died, and God Himself buried Moses.

When the people heard that their great leader had died, they wept and were sad for thirty days. Now Joshua became the leader, and the people listened to him and obeyed him.

Numbers 27:12-23; Deuteronomy 31:1 — 34:12

Gideon Surprises the Midianites

Gideon

The Children of Israel were living in the beautiful Land of Promise. There they had orchards and gardens and plenty of everything.

But they forgot the Lord, who had been so kind to them, and they began praying to an idol called Baal. This displeased God, and He punished His people by letting the Midianites come into their country.

These enemies took away their crops. They stole their sheep and their cattle. God's people became very poor; they even had to run away to the hills and hide in caves.

One day the Angel of the Lord came to a young man named Gideon. "The Lord is with you," said the Angel. "Go, and you will save Israel from the hand of the Midianites."

At first Gideon did not want to go, for he did not think he was able to do this great deed. But the Lord said: "I will be with you, and you shall win the victory over the Midianites."

Gideon now believed the promise of the Lord and gathered a large army. Then the Lord said: "You have too many soldiers. The people might become proud and say, 'My own hand has saved me.'"

So Gideon said that all who were afraid should go home again. Many of them went home, but the Lord said: "The people are still too many." Gideon kept on sending men home until he had only 300 of the bravest soldiers left.

Gideon divided these three hundred men into three companies. He gave each man a trumpet, a pitcher made of clay, and a burning torch. "Look at me," said Gideon, "and do whatever I do."

In the middle of the night, Gideon and his soldiers spread out in a big circle around the camp of the Midianites. Suddenly Gideon blew his trumpet. That was the signal.

The three hundred men blew their trumpets. They dashed their pitchers to the ground. They held up the burning torches. They cried: "The sword of the Lord and of Gideon!"

The Midianites now came running out of their tents. They saw the torches burning all around the camp. They thought a great army was there.

Eager to get away, they began killing one another in the darkness. Soon the men of Israel gathered and chased after the Midianites and killed them. God had fought for His people Israel.

He had sent Gideon to save them from the Midianites.

Judges 6:1-16, 33-35; 7:1-8, 15-23

Ruth

Ruth

Once there was a famine in the land of Israel. A man of Bethlehem and his wife Naomi moved to the land of Moab with their two sons. There the two sons married young women of Moab whose names were Orpah and Ruth. After a time the father died and also the two sons, and Naomi was left alone with Orpah and Ruth.

One day Naomi made up her mind to go back to Bethlehem, and Orpah and Ruth got ready and started off with her.

Soon Naomi stopped and said in her kind way: "Go back to your father's house," for she thought they would be happier with their parents. They all wept at the thought of parting. Then Orpah kissed Naomi and went back to the land of Moab.

But Ruth would not let Naomi go alone. "Ask me not to leave you," she said. "Where you go, I will go; where you stay, I will stay; your people shall be my people, and your God my God." Now Naomi took Ruth with her, and they came to Bethlehem at the beginning of the barley harvest.

Ruth knew that Naomi was very poor and had no one to care for her. Ruth loved Naomi. She would take care of her. "Let me go to the field and gather grain," she begged. Naomi let Ruth go, and she picked up ears of grain which the reapers let fall.

While Ruth was busy picking up grain, Boaz, the owner of the field, came out. He saw Ruth and asked the reapers who she was. They said: "It is the young woman who came back with Naomi. She has picked up grain all morning."

Boaz went to Ruth and said: "Do not go to gather grain in another field, but stay here; and when you are thirsty, drink from the water jar." Ruth made a low bow and asked: "Why are you so kind to me, a stranger?"

Boaz answered: "Because I have heard all you have done for Naomi and how you have left your own land to come here. May the Lord reward you."

All day Ruth picked up ears of grain, and in the evening she brought the grain home to Naomi.

After that she came every day to the field of Boaz until all the barley and wheat had been gathered. Later Boaz saw Ruth often.

He loved her and at last married her. God gave them a son, and they called his name Obed. He was the grandfather of King David, of whose family Jesus, our Savior, was born.

Ruth 1:1 – 4:22

Hannah Made a Special Coat for Samuel

Hannah and Samuel

Long ago there lived a good woman whose name was Hannah. Her husband's name was Elkanah. They had no children. This made Hannah sad, for she wanted very much to have a child.

Once every year Hannah and Elkanah went to the house of God in Shiloh. There they prayed and brought an offering to the Lord. One day when Hannah was in Shiloh, at the house of God, she was so sad that she cried and would not eat.

Her husband tried to comfort her, but she would not be comforted. She went into the house of God by herself and asked God to give her a boy baby. She also made a promise. She said: "Lord, if You will give me a son, I will give him back to serve You as long as he lives."

Eli, the priest, was sitting near by while Hannah prayed. He saw that her lips moved, but he did not hear her say anything. He wondered what was the matter.

Hannah was praying in her heart. She said to Eli: "I am a woman with a sad heart; I have told all my troubles to the Lord."

Eli was pleased and said: "Go in peace; may God give you what you have asked of Him."

Hannah went home with her husband. She was no longer sad. She ate and was happy, for she was sure that God would answer her prayer. Sometime afterward God answered Hannah's prayer. He gave her a son, and she was happy. She called him Samuel.

While the baby was very small, Hannah did not go to Shiloh. But she did not forget her promise to God. When Samuel was old enough, she brought him to the house of God.

She said to Eli, the priest: "I am the woman who prayed here. I prayed for this child, and God has answered my prayer; therefore I have lent him to the Lord. As long as he lives, he shall serve the Lord."

Hannah thanked God for her son; and after that she went home. But Samuel stayed in God's house. There he began serving the Lord as Eli's helper.

Every year Hannah came to the house of God in Shiloh, and each time she brought Samuel a new coat that she had made for him.

1 Samuel 1:1 — 2:19

43

David and Jonathan

David and Jonathan

Saul, the first king of Israel, raised an army to fight the Philistines, who wanted to make slaves of God's people. The Philistines had their camp on a mountain on one side of the valley, and Saul's soldiers gathered on a mountain on the other side.

Every morning and evening a giant named Goliath stood and cried to the soldiers of Saul: "Choose a man to fight with me; if he kills me, we will be your servants; if I kill him, you will be our servants." Not one of Saul's soldiers dared to go out and fight the giant.

One day a shepherd lad named David came to Saul and said: "I will go and fight the giant." "Go, and the Lord be with you," said King Saul. Goliath wore a suit of armor and carried a sword and a spear, and he trusted in himself.

David had nothing but a sling and five smooth stones, but he trusted in the Lord. Bravely he ran to meet the giant. He put a stone in his sling and let it fly straight to the forehead of Goliath, who fell down on his face. David then drew the giant's sword and killed him with it.

After David had killed Goliath, the captain of the army brought him to King Saul. At the palace Jonathan, the king's son, met David, and they became very dear friends. They promised always to be true to each other, and Jonathan gave David his robe and his sword and bow. King Saul would not let David go home again, but set him over his soldiers. Everyone loved David because he was such a brave soldier.

When the war with the Philistines was over, the women of all the cities came out to meet the soldiers. They were singing and dancing and said: "Saul has killed his thousands, and David his ten thousands." Saul also was there. He heard that they praised David more than him. This made him jealous of David and angry.

The next day an evil spirit came upon Saul as David played before him on the harp. Saul had a spear in his hand, and he threw the spear to kill David. But David got out of the way and ran off.

Now Saul tried other ways to kill David. He even told Jonathan and all his servants that they should kill David. Jonathan was David's friend, so he told David: "My father wants to kill you; go and hide yourself."

Jonathan also went to Saul and spoke well of David. "Do not sin against David," he said. "He even risked his life and killed Goliath." Saul listened to Jonathan and promised not to harm David.

Then for a while the king was friendly to David, but before long he tried a second time to kill him with a spear. Again David got away and hid outside the city.

When Jonathan again spoke well of David, the king became so angry that he threw his spear at Jonathan.

Now Jonathan knew that his father would keep on trying to kill David. He went to David's hiding place and told him. So they kissed each other and wept and said good-bye.

Then David went away to hide himself, and Jonathan returned to the palace.

1 Samuel 17:1 – 18:11; 19:1 – 20:42

David Spares King Saul's Life

David's Suffering Under Saul

David now lived in a wild, hilly country with about four hundred men who came out to him. One day Saul entered a cave in which David and some of his men were hiding. David cut off a piece of Saul's robe, but he would not let his men kill the king.

As soon as Saul had gone away from the cave, David came out and held up the piece of his robe. "Now you know I do not want to harm you," he said. David's kindness made Saul cry. "You have paid me good for evil," he said.

Saul went back to his home, but David and his men had to keep on living in the hills.

Saul tried once more to take David captive. This time David's spies saw where Saul's 3,000 soldiers were camping. Late at night David and Abishai stole into the camp. They found Saul fast asleep.

David would not let Abishai kill the king, but he told him to take Saul's spear and water jar. David called to the king from the top of a hill, and the king wept again and promised to quit hunting David.

Soon afterwards the Philistines defeated the Israelites in battle. Jonathan and his two brothers were killed, and Saul was badly hurt by an arrow. "Kill me with your sword," said Saul to his armor-bearer. When the man refused, Saul fell on his own sword and died.

David wept when he learned of the death of Saul and Jonathan. But he was now able to go back to his home again. The people also came and made him their new king.

And he was a good king. He served the Lord and led the people to serve the Lord and obey His commandments. His sufferings helped to make him a good king.

1 Samuel 22:1 – 31:13; 2 Samuel 1:1 – 5:5

Solomon at the Altar of the Temple

The Building of the Temple

For more than four hundred years the Children of Israel had no church except the Tabernacle, a big tent, where the ark of God was kept. David was not allowed to build the Temple, but he gathered much gold and silver and many other things which Solomon, his son, could use.

Solomon was king four years when he began planning the Temple. He followed a pattern David had given him from the Lord. The work of building took seven years. Many workmen had to cut big cedar trees, others had to cut stones, others had to work with gold, silver, and brass.

The Temple was built of large stones. As soon as the walls and the roof were up, the inside was covered with cedar boards. Thin sheets of bright gold were spread over the walls, the ceiling, and the floor. The walls and the doors were decorated with figures of angels, palm trees, and flowers.

The Temple was divided into two parts. One part was called the Holy of Holies. It was for the ark of God and was always dark.

In it stood two angels made of wood and covered with gold. They faced each other and looked down on the ark. They were fifteen feet high, and their wings were spread out.

The other part of the Temple was called the Holy Place. It had a golden altar for incense, a table made of gold for showbread, and ten golden candlesticks.

The showbread was twelve loaves of bread laid before the Lord. The bread was changed every Sabbath day. Between the two parts of the Temple hung a pretty curtain of many colors with figures of angels woven in it.

Outside the Temple was an open space called the court. It had a big altar, on which the sacrifices were burned, and a large basin full of water.

Solomon invited all the people to Jerusalem for the first service, and the Lord showed that He was pleased by filling the whole Temple with a thick cloud.

Solomon knelt before the altar and asked God to look down in mercy on this house of His, to hear the prayers of the people, and always to be with His people. Solomon also blessed the people, saying: "The Lord be with us as He was with our fathers. Let Him not leave us, that we may keep His commandments."

After that Solomon offered many sacrifices, and all the people held a feast with him. The people went home joyful and glad of heart, because the Lord had been so kind and good to Israel.

1 Kings 5:1-18; 8:1-66

Elijah and the Ravens

Elijah

Many years after Solomon died, a man named Ahab became king. He was one of the wickedest kings that ever ruled over God's people Israel.

Ahab married the heathen princess Jezebel, who was even more wicked than the king. She prayed to an idol called Baal. She paid many priests to serve Baal and to make the people pray to this false god.

One day God sent the great prophet Elijah to King Ahab. Elijah said to Ahab: "As the Lord God of Israel lives, whose servant I am, there shall be no dew nor rain during these years."

Then Elijah went away and lived by a brook near the Jordan River, for so God had said he should. "You are to drink water from the brook," God said, "and I have told the ravens to feed you." Every morning and every evening these birds brought him bread and meat, and when he was thirsty, he drank water from the brook.

After a while the brook dried up because there had been no rain. Now God sent Elijah to a town in a heathen land, saying:

"I have told a widow there to feed you." So he arose and went to this land.

When Elijah came to the gate of the town, the widow was there, gathering sticks to make a fire. "Please bring me a little water that I may drink," said the prophet.

As she was going to get it, he called to her and said: "Bring me a little piece of bread."

She answered: "I have only a handful of flour in a jar and a little olive oil in a bottle. I am gathering sticks that I may bake it for me and my son, and then we must die."

"Fear not," said Elijah. "Go and do as you have said. But make me a little cake first; for the Lord God of Israel says: 'The flour in the jar will not be used up until the day the Lord sends rain.'"

The widow now did as Elijah had said, and the word of the Lord which the prophet had spoken came true.

Every day for a long time she and her son and Elijah had food, until the Lord sent rain.

1 Kings 16:29-33; 17:1-16

Naaman's Maid

Naaman and Elisha

In the days of Elisha a great man, named Naaman, lived in the land of Syria. He was captain of the king's army and had won many battles. But Naaman had a dreadful sickness. No doctor could heal him.

At one time the army of Syria had made war against God's people Israel. They had taken a little girl from her home and brought her to their own land. Here she became a helper to Naaman's wife.

One day the little girl said: "I wish my master were with the prophet in the land of Israel. He would heal him of his sickness." Naaman's wife told her husband what the girl had said.

When the king of Syria heard of it, he said: "Go to the prophet, and I will send a letter to the king of Israel." Naaman went and took costly presents with him.

He also brought the letter to the king of Israel. When the king read the letter, he became afraid and did not know what to do. But Elisha heard what had happened. "Let him come to me," he said.

So Naaman came with his horses and chariots and stood at the door of Elisha's house.

But Elisha did not come out to see Naaman. No, he sent a man to tell him: "Go and wash in the Jordan River seven times, and you will be cured."

Naaman became angry. He thought the prophet should come out and pray to his God and heal him. He turned around and went away.

But his servants said to him: "Why not do as the prophet told you?" Then Naaman went down and dipped himself seven times in the Jordan River. When he came out of the water, he was healed.

At once Naaman went back to Elisha's house. He said to the prophet: "Now I know that there is no God anywhere but in Israel." He wanted to give Elisha the presents, but Elisha would not take anything. "Go in peace," he said to the captain. So Naaman went home with a glad heart.

2 Kings 5:1-27

The Four Lepers Found Food in the Forsaken
Camp of the Syrians

The Four Lepers of Samaria

Once, long ago, the king of Syria came to the city of Samaria with a large army. The city gates were closed up tight, so the enemy soldiers camped around the city. No one could get in or out, and no food could be brought into the city.

Soon there was less and less food left in the city. Food began to cost so much that few people could buy any. The king of Israel also lived in Samaria. He saw how his people had to suffer. He blamed Elisha, God's prophet, who did not want the people to give up the city to the enemy.

When the king and his men came to talk to Elisha, Elisha said: "Hear the word of the Lord. Tomorrow about this time there will be plenty of food for everyone."

That evening four lepers who lived near the gate of the city decided to hunt for some food. They knew they couldn't get any in the starving city, so they decided to go to the camp of the Syrian army. They didn't care what would happen to them.

When they reached the camp, they found that the enemy soldiers had fled, leaving everything behind them. God had made the Syrian army hear the noise of chariots and horses, and the soldiers had run away in fear.

In the tents the lepers found great amounts of food and drink. After they had eaten, they also took some gold and silver and some clothing and hid these things.

About that time they began to be ashamed of being selfish, and decided to share the good news. So they went and told the king that there was plenty of food for all in the camp of the Syrians.

The king of Israel listened to their story and sent several of his men to see for themselves. They found that the lepers had spoken the truth.

Now the hungry people of the city rushed to the enemy camp and brought plenty of food and other supplies back to the city.

In this way God gave them what they needed; He kept the promise He had made through Elisha, His prophet.

2 Kings 6:24 – 7:20

Jonah Preaching to the People of Nineveh

The Story of Jonah

Long ago there was a prophet whose name was Jonah. God told this prophet to preach to a great heathen city called Nineveh. Jonah did not want to go to those people because they were heathen.

Instead of going to Nineveh he went to the sea and got on a ship that was sailing in the opposite way. But God was watching him.

As the ship was sailing along, God sent a very bad storm. The ship was about to break into pieces. The sailors threw out all of the goods to make the ship lighter, but the storm grew worse. Then every sailor prayed to his god for help. Still the storm kept on.

All this time Jonah was sleeping down below in the ship. The captain came to him and said: "Get up and pray to your God, perhaps He will save us."

The sailors thought that someone on the ship might have done a great wrong. They cast lots to find out who it could be, and the lot fell on Jonah.

Now Jonah had to tell them what he had done. He told them he was trying to run away from God. He also said: "Throw me into the sea, and the storm will stop." The sailors did not want to do this, but the storm grew worse.

At last they took Jonah and threw him into the sea. Then the wind stopped blowing right away. When the sailors saw this, they feared the God of Jonah and offered sacrifices to Him.

God did not forget about Jonah. He sent a big fish to where Jonah was thrown into the sea, and this fish swallowed Jonah whole.

For three days and three nights Jonah was in this fish. There he thought about his sins and began to pray to God. Then God spoke to the fish, and the fish came near the shore and spit Jonah up on dry land.

Once more God told Jonah to go to Nineveh. This time Jonah went. Nineveh was a very big city, and its people were very wicked. When Jonah came into the city, he began to preach. "In 40 days Nineveh will be destroyed," he said.

The people and the king believed Jonah's message was from God and were sorry for having sinned. They prayed to the God of Jonah and brought sacrifices, hoping that He would have mercy on them.

God saw that the people of Nineveh were giving up their sinful ways. He took pity on them and did not destroy the city.

God is willing to forgive sins whenever people repent. Jonah helped to save the people of Nineveh by bringing them God's Word.

Jonah 1:1 — 4:11

Hezekiah Took the Letter into the Temple and
Showed It to God

Hezekiah

Hezekiah was a good king. He lived in Jerusalem. But he had strong and wicked enemies. One of them was Sennacherib, king of Assyria. Sennacherib was making war on many cities and countries and was winning.

Good King Hezekiah did not have a big army as his enemy had. But when Sennacherib came toward the city of Jerusalem, Hezekiah prayed to the Lord, who is able to help His people in any trouble.

Hezekiah also sent a message to the prophet Isaiah and asked him to pray for his country. The prophet sent a cheerful message back to the king. "Do not be afraid," he said, "God will drive the enemy away."

One day Sennacherib sent some of his men to Jerusalem. They shouted to the people that Hezekiah was fooling them and that God would not help them.

Sennacherib also sent a letter in which he made fun of Isaiah and God. Hezekiah took the letter into the temple and showed it to God in prayer. He said: "O Lord God, You have made heaven and earth; save us from the enemy."

The Lord answered Hezekiah's prayer. He had His prophet Isaiah send another message to Hezekiah. It said, "Thus says the Lord. 'Sennacherib shall not come into this city, nor shoot an arrow into it, for I will defend this city.'"

That same night the angel of the Lord went to the camp of the Assyrians and killed 185,000 of Sennacherib's soldiers. So that wicked king had to flee back to his own country. There, as he was praying to his idols, his own sons killed him with a sword.

Some time later King Hezekiah was in bed, very sick. God sent the prophet Isaiah to tell him that it was time for him to die. When Hezekiah heard this, he turned to the wall and cried. "I beg You, O Lord," he prayed, "to let me live a little longer."

Again God heard the king's prayer. Isaiah was just leaving when God told him to go back to the king. "Tell Hezekiah," said God, "I have heard your prayer; I have seen your tears.

"I will heal you and will add 15 years to your life." That same day good King Hezekiah got well. For 15 more years he ruled over God's people.

2 Kings 18:1 — 20:21

The Priest Reads from God's Book

Josiah, the Royal Reformer

Josiah was made king over God's people when he was only eight years old. While he was young, some good men taught him to serve the Lord and helped him rule the people.

The Bible says: "Josiah did that which was right in the sight of the Lord and walked in all the ways of David, his father, and turned not aside to the right or to the left."

But most of the people were not good like their king. They prayed to idols and did many other wicked things that displeased the Lord. The Temple that Solomon had built was no longer clean and beautiful because very few people loved the Lord and His house.

Some of the stones were falling out of the walls, the boards were rotting away, and inside it was full of rubbish.

When Josiah was a young man, he said to his servant: "Go to the high priest and tell him to have workmen repair the Temple and make it beautiful again." The servant went at once to the temple, and there he had a great surprise. "I have found the Book of God," said the high priest.

This Book had been lying there forgotten for many years because the people no longer cared to learn God's Word. The servant returned to the king, carrying the Book under his arm.

He told Josiah that the Temple was being cleaned and made beautiful again. He also opened the Book and read some parts of it to him.

King Josiah felt very sad because God's Book said that the Lord would send a terrible punishment upon His people if they prayed to idols and did not obey His commandments.

He sent for the priests and prophets and all the people and had them meet with him in the Temple at Jerusalem. One of the priests arose and read to the people from the Book of God that had been lost and found again.

As soon as the priest had finished reading, the king stood up before all the people and made a promise to the Lord to obey all His commandments. The people also promised the Lord that they would quit doing wickedly and would keep God's commandments.

Some of the wicked kings who lived before Josiah's time had put up altars to idols in the Temple and on high places near the city of Jerusalem. All over the land there were high places with altars and idols.

Josiah commanded his men to pull down the altars and idols and to burn them. They went from place to place, and wherever they found idols, they ground them to powder and burned them.

So good King Josiah had the Temple cleaned and made beautiful again. He burned the idols and taught the people to worship the Lord only. As long as he lived, he kept the promise he had made to obey the commandments of the Lord.

2 Kings 22:1-13; 23:1-25

Daniel and His Friends

Daniel and His Three Friends

When Daniel was a boy, he first lived in the land of Judah. But the people in his country had become very wicked, so God allowed Nebuchadnezzar, the king of Babylon, to take their country.

Nebuchadnezzar's soldiers burned Jerusalem and the Temple and took a number of the people back with them to Babylon. Among the captives were Daniel and his three friends, Shadrach, Meshach, and Abednego.

King Nebuchadnezzar decided to train some of his younger captives for service to him. They were to receive a special education. They were to have the best teachers.

Since the king also wanted them to grow strong and healthy, he ordered for these students the same meat and wine which he received.

Daniel and his three friends knew that some of the king's food had been offered to idols and that God did not want them to eat it. Daniel was eager to obey God and to do nothing that would displease God.

So he asked the king's servant to excuse him and his three friends from eating the king's food. The king's servant was afraid of disobeying the king. He said: "When you appear before the king and will not look as well as your companions, the king may kill me."

Daniel answered: "Try it, I beg you, for 10 days. Give us vegetables to eat and water to drink. At the end of that time compare our faces with those of the others, and whatever is best you may then do."

The servant agreed, and at the end of 10 days Daniel and his three friends looked better than any of their companions. After that the king's servant gave them vegetables every day.

During their three-year training period God blessed Daniel and his friends for being faithful to Him. He gave them much knowledge and wisdom. Daniel also was able to understand dreams.

At the end of the three years all students had to appear before the king. When King Nebuchadnezzar questioned them, he found none that were as wise as Daniel, Shadrach, Meshach, and Abednego. They were 10 times wiser than all the wise men of the country.

Daniel 1:1-20

Shadrach, Meshach, and Abednego Did Not Bow Down
to the Idol

The Three Men in the Fiery Furnace

King Nebuchadnezzar did not believe in the true God, but prayed to idols.

At one time this king made a big image of gold. He said all the people should fall down and pray to the image. But there were three men who prayed only to the true God. They were Shadrach, Meshach, and Abednego, the friends of Daniel.

When the king heard that they would not fall down and pray to the image, he became very angry. He called the three men and said: "If you do not pray to the image, I will throw you into a burning, fiery furnace; and who is that God who will save you?"

The three men answered: "Our God is able to save us from the fiery furnace. Even if He does not, we will not serve your gods nor pray to the golden image."

This answer made the king still more angry. He told the people to make the furnace seven times hotter than at other times.

He sent his strongest soldiers to tie these three men and to throw them into the furnace. It was so hot that the heat killed the soldiers who threw the three men into the fire.

Soon the king began to be afraid, for when he looked into the furnace, he did not see *three* men but *four!* They were not tied! They were walking loose in the fire! And they were not burned! The fourth man was an angel. God had sent him to keep the three men from being hurt by the fire.

The king called to the three brave men. He said: "You servants of the most high God, come out of the furnace." The three men came out of the fire. They were not burned. Not even their hair had caught fire, and there was no smell of fire on their clothes.

The king said: "Blessed be the God who has sent His angel and saved His servants who trusted in Him!" He passed a law that any man who would say anything against the true God should be put to death. Then he made these three men some of his highest officers.

Daniel 3:1-30

Daniel in the Lions' Den

Daniel in the Lions' Den

The king of Babylon put princes over his kingdom. Over the princes he put three presidents. The highest of these was Daniel, a prophet of the true God.

Daniel was a very good president. He did his work well and always prayed to the true God. But the other presidents became jealous of Daniel. They wanted to get him out of the way. They asked the king to make a wicked law.

For thirty days no one was to pray to any god, but only to the king. Anyone who did not obey this law was to be thrown into a den of lions. The king did not know that these men wanted to get rid of Daniel; so he made the law.

Daniel knew that the king had made this wicked law. But he kept on praying to the true God as he had always done. Three times a day he got on his knees before his window and prayed.

The princes sent spies to watch Daniel. On the very first day they found him praying to God. They went to the king and said:

"Daniel prays to his God three times a day. You must throw him into the den of lions!"

Now the king was very sorry. But because he had made the law, he thought he had to put Daniel into the den of hungry lions, and he did so.

All night long the king thought about Daniel and could not sleep. In the morning he got up very early and went to the lions' den. "O Daniel," he called, "is your God, whom you serve all the time, able to save you from the lions?"

Daniel answered: "My God has sent His angel and has shut the lions' mouths, and they have not hurt me."

The king was glad when he heard Daniel's voice. He told his servants to take Daniel out of the den. Now Daniel's enemies were thrown into the den, and the lions killed them before they touched the ground.

But Daniel was not hurt at all, because he had trusted in God.

Daniel 6:1-28

Rebuilding the Walls of Jerusalem

Ezra and Nehemiah

Because of the wickedness of His people God let a heathen king and his soldiers burn the city of Jerusalem and the beautiful Temple. Many of the people were taken to another land.

At the end of seventy years Cyrus, a king who knew God, told the people that they could return to their homeland. Led by two brave men, a large number of them returned to Jerusalem.

The first thing they did when they came to Jerusalem was to build an altar on which to offer sacrifices to the Lord. Then they began building houses for themselves, and they started rebuilding the Temple.

But the enemies who lived around the city caused them so much trouble that twenty years passed before the Temple was finished. It was not nearly as beautiful as the Temple Solomon had built. But the people knew that it was God's house, so they had a special holiday on which they praised the Lord with songs and musical instruments.

Many years later a priest named Ezra arrived in Jerusalem with more of God's people. Ezra had a deep understanding of God's Word. He taught God's Word to the people. He told them they must repent of their sins if they wanted God to bless them.

In a faraway land lived Nehemiah, a godly person, who was the king's cupbearer. He heard that the walls of Jerusalem were still broken down and that the people were not safe from their enemies.

The king saw that he was sad. When he learned the reason for it, he said Nehemiah could go to Jerusalem and help his people.

After a long journey Nehemiah came to Jerusalem. He and Ezra gathered the people together to hear God's Word. Ezra and many other priests stood on a raised platform. Ezra read God's Word to the people all morning, and the other priests explained it.

The people found out from God's Word how they had sinned, and they wept. But the priests told them they should eat and drink and be happy, because the Lord had forgiven their sins.

Nehemiah was the leader of the people in building the walls of the city. Their enemies gathered daily and mocked them. They even wanted to come with weapons and stop them.

But Nehemiah placed soldiers on guard and told the builders to carry their swords and be ready to fight. At last the walls were finished, and the gates were built. Now there was another holiday on which the people blew trumpets and thanked God.

Ezra 1:1 – 3:13; Nehemiah 4:1 – 12:43

The Angel Gabriel and Zacharias

Zacharias

In the days when Herod was king over the land of God's people, there lived a priest named Zacharias. The name of his wife was Elizabeth.

They were both good people, who believed in the promised Savior and did what pleased the heavenly Father. But they had no child, and both of them were now very old.

One day Zacharias was in the holy place of the Temple, burning incense on a little golden altar. All at once an angel stood there at the side of the altar.

It was the angel Gabriel. Zacharias was very much afraid. But the angel said, "Do not be afraid, Zacharias, for God has heard your prayer. Your wife, Elizabeth, will be the mother of a son, and you are to call him John. He will have the Holy Spirit and will get the people ready for the coming of Jesus, the Savior."

This was too wonderful for Zacharias to believe at once. So he said: "How shall I know these things?" The angel said to Zacharias: "Because you did not believe my words, you will not be able to speak until the little boy is born."

All this time the people waited outside. They wondered why the priest did not come out to bless them and to send them home.

When he did come, they knew at once that something strange had happened. For Zacharias made signs with his hands, but was not able to speak a word.

Soon afterwards Zacharias was finished serving in the Temple and went back to his home.

Luke 1:5-25

Mary and the Angel Gabriel

Mary

In the city of Nazareth lived a young woman whose name was Mary. She was soon to be married to a man named Joseph. Mary and Joseph were both related to the great King David, but they were poor people.

One day the angel Gabriel came to Mary and said: "Greetings! The Lord is with you." When Mary saw the angel, she was afraid and wondered what his words meant.

"Do not be afraid, Mary," said the angel, "for God is pleased with you. You shall have a Son, and you are to call Him Jesus. He shall be great and shall be called the Son of the Highest. He shall be a King and shall rule over His people forever."

"How shall I have a son, when I am not living with a husband?" asked Mary. The angel answered: "The Holy Spirit shall come upon you; for that reason your Son shall be called the Son of God."

The angel also said: "With God nothing shall be impossible." Mary said: "I am God's servant. Let it be with me as you have said." Then the angel went away.

After this, Mary left her home and hurried off to visit her cousin Elizabeth. She believed the angel's words.

She was very happy to know that God would soon send the Savior. She was glad that she would be the mother of the Savior.

During her visit with Elizabeth she sang a beautiful song of praise. Mary stayed with Elizabeth three months before going back to her home in Nazareth.

Luke 1:26-56

Zacharias Writing on the Slate

The Birth of John the Baptizer

Elizabeth was very happy when she knew that God was going to give her a son in her old age. After some time the words of the angel came true.

Elizabeth became the mother of a baby boy. Not only Zacharias and Elizabeth, but also their neighbors and relatives were glad when they heard how good the Lord had been to Elizabeth.

On the eighth day after his birth the baby was to be given a name. All the friends began calling him Zacharias, after his father.

But the mother said: "No, he shall be called John." They were surprised and said: "None of your relatives has that name."

Then they asked the father to tell them what name the baby should have. Zacharias had them bring him a slate, and he wrote on the slate, "His name is John."

As Zacharias was writing, he suddenly was able to speak again. At once he began to praise God. All the people were much surprised. They wondered what the baby would be when he grew up.

When John grew up, he became a preacher. He preached to the people, and told them to turn away from their sins and to wait for the Savior.

He said the Savior would come soon to teach them and to save them from their sins. He also baptized all who were sorry for their sins and believed in the promised Savior.

Because he baptized the people, he is called John the Baptizer.

Luke 1:57-80; 3:1-6

The Birth of Jesus

The Birth of Our Savior

Mary was not yet living with Joseph when the angel told her she was to be the mother of God's Son. But one night an angel came to Joseph in a dream and said: "Do not be afraid to take Mary to be your wife.

"She will be the mother of a Son, and you are to name Him Jesus; for He shall save His people from their sins." When Joseph awoke, He took Mary into his own home and cared for her.

Joseph and Mary lived in Nazareth. But Micah, a man of God, had said long before that *Bethlehem* would be the Savior's birthplace. Now this is how God planned to have His Son born in Bethlehem.

The Romans ruled over many lands, also over the land where Mary and Joseph lived. Augustus, the Roman ruler, made a law that all the people in his lands should have their names written in his books.

He wanted to show how much tax each person was to pay. Everyone had to go to the place where the names of his family and relatives were kept in one of the books. Joseph and Mary were relatives of King David, and the book with the names of David's relatives was in Bethlehem.

Joseph and Mary got ready and traveled the long way (about 120 miles) from Nazareth to Bethlehem. That is how the words of Micah, the man of God, came true. That is why Joseph and Mary were in Bethlehem when Jesus was born. Now read the story as it is told in the Bible:

"And it came to pass in those days that there went out a decree (law) from Caesar Augustus that all the world should be taxed. And all went to be taxed, everyone into his own city.

"And Joseph also went up from Galilee, out of the city of Nazareth, into Judea, unto the city of David, which is called Bethlehem, because he was of the house (family) of David, to be taxed with Mary.

"And so it was that while they were there, the days were accomplished (the time came) that she should be delivered (her child should be born).

"And she brought forth her first-born Son and wrapped Him in swaddling clothes and laid Him in a manger, because there was no room for them in the inn."

Matthew 1:18-24; Luke 2:1-7

The Shepherds Receiving the News of Jesus' Birth

The Announcement to the Shepherds

After the baby Jesus was born, some of God's angels came to tell people about His birth. The Bible tells the story in these words:

"And there were in the same country shepherds abiding (staying) in the field, keeping watch over their flock by night. And, lo, the angel of the Lord came upon them, and the glory of the Lord shone round about them; and they were sore afraid.

"And the angel said unto them: 'Fear not; for behold, I bring you good tidings (news) of great joy, which shall be to all people. For unto you is born this day in the city of David a Savior, which is Christ the Lord. And this shall be a sign unto you: ye shall find the Babe wrapped in swaddling clothes, lying in a manger.'

"And suddenly there was with the angel a multitude of the heavenly host (angels), praising God and saying: 'Glory to God in the highest, and on earth peace, good will toward men!'

"And it came to pass, as the angels were gone away from them into heaven, the shepherds said one to another: 'Let us now go even unto Bethlehem and see this thing which is come to pass, which the Lord hath made known unto us.'

"And they came with haste and found Mary and Joseph, and the Babe lying in a manger.

"And when they had seen it, they made known abroad the saying which was told them concerning this Child.

"And all they that heard it wondered at those things which were told them by the shepherds.

"But Mary kept all these things and pondered them in her heart.

"And the shepherds returned, glorifying and praising God for all the things that they had heard and seen, as it was told unto them."

Luke 2:8-20

Simeon and the Baby Jesus

The Presentation of Jesus

The people of God who lived long ago had the Ten Commandments, but they also had certain other laws, or commandments, that God wanted them to obey.

One of these laws said that parents should bring their first boy baby to their church and give him to the Lord.

Joseph and Mary were careful to obey God's laws. So, when Jesus was forty days old, they brought Him to the Temple in Jerusalem. There they gave Him to the Lord.

Then Mary also brought a sacrifice. Since she was poor, she could not bring a lamb, so she brought two young pigeons.

The same day there was an old man named Simeon in the temple. He was a good man who had waited long for the coming of the Savior.

When Simeon saw the baby Jesus, he took Him in his arms, and he thanked God for letting him see the Savior. He prayed, telling God that he was ready to die.

After this, Simeon told Mary and Joseph some things that would happen. He said that Jesus would save all people from sin.

He also said that someday Mary would have great sorrow, for Jesus would die on the cross to save all people.

Besides Simeon, there was an old woman in the temple. Her name was Anna. She stayed in the temple night and day and spent her time in prayer.

Anna saw Jesus and she thanked God for sending Him. She also told the people who were there that this Baby was the Savior of the world.

After this, Mary and Joseph took the baby Jesus back to their home in Bethlehem.

Luke 2:21-40

The Wise Men Come to Bring Gifts to Jesus

The Wise Men

About the time when Jesus was born God put a very special star into the sky. Some Wise Men who lived far away in the East saw the star, and they knew that Jesus, their King, had been born. They said they would go and find Jesus.

The Wise Men got ready, and soon they were on their way. They rode many days. At last they came to Jerusalem.

The Wise Men asked some people: "Where is the new King? We have seen His star in the East. We have come to worship Him." But no one could tell them where the new King was.

An evil king lived in Jerusalem. His name was Herod. When he heard that a new King had been born, he became worried. He said to himself, "So, someone wants to be king in my place! I will kill this new King."

Herod asked some teachers where Jesus was to be born. "In Bethlehem," they said.

Then Herod called the Wise Men and said:

"Go to Bethlehem and look for the Child. When you have found Him, come back to me and tell me where He is, so that I may go and pray to Him also."

Herod did not tell the truth when he said this. He really wanted to kill Jesus.

The Wise Men started on their way to Bethlehem. They were glad when they saw the star again. It went before them and stood over the house where Jesus was.

There the Wise Men went into the house and found Jesus. They were very happy. They prayed to Jesus. Kneeling down before Jesus, they gave Him gold and other rich gifts.

Then they were ready to go home. Before they started on their way, God spoke to them. He said: "Do not go back to Herod. Go home another way."

The Wise Men obeyed God and did not return to tell wicked Herod where Jesus was.

Matthew 2:1-12

Mary, Baby Jesus, and Joseph Travel to Egypt

The Flight to Egypt

Soon after the Wise Men had gone home, God sent an angel to Joseph in a dream.

The angel said: "Arise, take the young Child and His mother, and hurry to Egypt. Stay there until I tell you to come back. Herod will soon look for the newborn King and will try to kill Him."

Then Joseph got up at once and took the Baby and His mother away quickly in the night. For many days and nights they traveled until they came to the country called Egypt.

When Herod saw that the Wise Men were not coming back to tell him where the new King was, he became very angry.

He sent his soldiers to Bethlehem and ordered them to kill all the babies who were two years old or younger.

In this cruel way King Herod thought he would surely put the new King to death. But someone stronger and wiser than Herod was watching over Jesus.

God soon punished Herod by having him die. After Herod was dead, God sent an angel to Joseph in Egypt.

The angel said to Joseph: "Now take the young Child, and go back to your country, for the wicked people who wanted to kill Him are dead."

So Joseph took Mary and Jesus back to the land of Israel. But because Herod's son was now king, Joseph went to his old home in Galilee instead of to Bethlehem.

There he and Mary and Jesus lived safely in a little town called Nazareth.

Matthew 2:13-23

The Boy Jesus with His Parents Going to Jerusalem

The Boy Jesus in the Temple

Every year in the springtime the people of the land where Jesus lived had a great church service in the Temple. They called it the Passover.

At this service they thanked God for the wonderful way in which He brought their people out of Egypt many years before.

Large crowds went to Jerusalem and to the beautiful Temple for the service. Mary and Joseph lived far away in Nazareth, but every year they went there, too. When Jesus was twelve years old, they took Him with them.

The service lasted seven days. At the close of the service, everyone went home again.

Mary and Joseph also started for home. Jesus, however, stayed in Jerusalem. Mary and Joseph did not know this, but they were not worried, for they thought Jesus was on the road with friends and relatives who were going the same way.

In the evening they began to look for Him.

They could not find Him along the road, so the next morning they went all the way back to Jerusalem and looked for Him there.

After three days they found Jesus in the Temple. He was sitting among some Bible teachers, listening to them and asking them questions. All who heard Jesus were surprised at how well He knew the Bible.

Mary said to Jesus: "Son, why have You done this to us? Your father and I have been looking for You."

Jesus said to His mother: "Why did you look for Me? Didn't you know that I must be doing My Father's work?"

Then Jesus went home with His parents and obeyed them. He grew bigger every day; He learned His lessons well; He obeyed God's commandments; and all the people who knew Him loved Him.

God the heavenly Father loved Him, too.

Luke 2:41-52

The Baptism of Jesus

The Baptism of Jesus

After Jesus had been in Jerusalem at the age of twelve, He lived in Nazareth eighteen years. During these years He studied and prayed. In this way He got ready to do the work for which the heavenly Father had sent Him.

When Jesus was about thirty years old, a man named John lived in a desert near the Jordan River. His clothing and food were strange. He wore a coat made of camel's hair, and he ate grasshoppers and wild honey.

God had sent John into the desert. He wanted him to preach there and get the people ready for the coming of the Savior. Large crowds came to hear John. They came from Jerusalem and from Judea and from all the country round about the Jordan River.

John said to the people: "Be sorry for your sins, and ask God to forgive you." Many who heard him were sorry for their sins.

One day Jesus came to the place where John was preaching and baptizing. He asked John to baptize Him also. At first John did not want to baptize Jesus. But Jesus said: "Let it be so now, for it is God's will."

Then Jesus stepped into the river, and John baptized Him.

After Jesus had been baptized, He came out of the water and prayed. While He was praying, a wonderful thing happened. The sky opened, and the Holy Spirit came down as a dove and settled on Jesus.

And a voice from heaven said: "This is My beloved Son, in whom I am well pleased."

The heavenly Father was pleased with Jesus because He was willing to obey Him in all things.

Matthew 3:1-17

Jesus Tells the Servants to Fill the Water Pots

The Wedding at Cana

After Jesus had been baptized, He was ready to begin His work. He gathered some men to follow Him and learn from Him. We call these men disciples.

Jesus went with His disciples to many places. Everywhere He went He taught the people that He was the Son of God and the Savior from sin.

A few days after Jesus had gathered the first of His disciples, He went to a wedding. This wedding was in a small town called Cana. The disciples went with Jesus.

Mary, the mother of Jesus, was at the wedding. Many other people were there, too.

Wine was served, but there was not enough for all the people. Soon it was all used up. Mary knew about the trouble. She went to Jesus for help. She said: "They have no wine."

Jesus said to His mother: "My time to help has not yet come."

Mary believed that Jesus would help. So she went to the servants and said: "Do whatever He tells you."

Six large waterpots stood along a wall of the house. The people kept water in the pots for washing and drinking. Jesus said to the servants: "Fill the waterpots with water."

The servants got water and filled them to the top.

Jesus now said to them: "Take some out and bring it to the man in charge of the feast."

When the servants did as Jesus told them, they saw that Jesus had done a wonderful thing—a miracle. He had changed water into wine!

The man in charge of the feast tasted the new wine and found that it was very good. He did not know where it had come from.

He called the man who had just been married and said: "Other people serve the best wine first, but you have kept the best wine until now."

Changing water into wine was the first miracle that Jesus did. By this miracle He proved that He is the Son of God, and His disciples believed in Him.

John 2:1-11

Nicodemus Visits Jesus at Night

Nicodemus

While Jesus was in Jerusalem, many people believed in Him because they saw the miracles He was doing. He healed many that were sick and blind and crippled.

One night a Pharisee, a ruler of the people, came to Jesus. His name was Nicodemus. He had heard about the miracles Jesus had done. He was sure that Jesus must be a very wise and great man. He wanted to talk to Jesus.

But Nicodemus was afraid to follow Jesus and go to Him when others would see him. Many of his friends hated Jesus. That is probably why Nicodemus went to visit Jesus after dark.

Nicodemus said to Jesus: "Master, we know that You are a Teacher who has come from God. No one can do the miracles You are doing unless God is with Him."

Jesus knew that Nicodemus had come to learn about living with God in His kingdom. "I tell you the truth," said Jesus, "unless a person is born again, he cannot see the kingdom of God."

At first Nicodemus could not understand what Jesus meant. He said: "How can a man be born when he is old?" Jesus answered: "I tell you the truth, only if a person is born by water and the Spirit can he come into the kingdom of God."

Jesus meant that only those who have their sins washed away and receive God's Spirit become His children and live with Him in His kingdom.

Nicodemus still was puzzled. He said: "How is this possible?" Jesus answered: "Are you a teacher and do not know this? We say what we know. And as Moses lifted up the snake in the desert, even so must the Son of Man be lifted up, that whosoever believeth in Him should not perish but have eternal life."

Jesus was telling how He would suffer and die on the cross so that all people could have forgiveness of sins and eternal life.

Then He said the best-known words in the Bible: "For God so loved the world that He gave His only-begotten Son, that whosoever believeth in Him should not perish, but have everlasting life."

People become children of God when the Holy Spirit gives them faith in Jesus, their Savior, who died for them. God's children live with Him both now and forever.

John 3:1-16

The Nobleman and His Son

Jesus Heals the Nobleman's Son

In the land where Jesus lived there was a happy family—a father, a mother, and a little boy. But one day the boy became sick. Day by day he grew worse, and his father and mother were very much worried about him.

Soon the boy was so sick that they thought he would never get well again.

Someone told the father that Jesus was in a city not very far away. So he went to Jesus as quickly as he could to pray for his son. When he met Jesus, he said: "Come and heal my son. He is dying."

Jesus said: "If you do not see miracles, you will not believe in Me."

The father prayed again, saying: "Lord, come, before my child dies."

Then Jesus spoke kindly to the man. He said: "Go on your way home. Your son is well."

The next day, while the father was on his way home, some servants met him. They said: "Your son is well."

The father asked what time his son began to get better. The servants answered: "Yesterday at one o'clock."

The father remembered that one o'clock was exactly the time when Jesus had said, "Your son is well."

John 4:43-54

"Rise Up, Take Up Your Pallet, and Walk"

The Healing of the Man at the Pool of Bethesda

In the great city of Jerusalem was a pool called Bethesda. Around the pool were five porches, and on them lay many people who were sick or blind or lame.

At certain times the water would bubble. The sick people would then step into the water. They believed that whoever stepped in first after the water had bubbled became well.

One day Jesus came to Jerusalem and went by the pool of Bethesda. He saw a man lying there who had been sick 38 years. Jesus went up to him and said: "Would you like to get well?" The man looked up at Jesus and answered: "Lord, I have no one to put me into the pool when the water is stirred. While I go, someone steps in ahead of me."

Jesus felt sorry for the man. He said: "Rise, take up your pallet, and walk." At once the man became perfectly well, got up, took his pallet, and began to walk.

As the happy man walked around, carrying the pallet, the leaders of the people saw him. "It is not right for you to carry your bed," they said to him; "today is the Sabbath."

They had a strict rule against doing any work on the Sabbath day. But the man replied: "The one who made me well told me, 'Take up your pallet and walk.'"

"Who is it," they asked, "that said to you, 'Take up your pallet and walk'?" But the man who had been made well did not know who it was because Jesus had disappeared in the crowd.

Later, however, Jesus found the man in the temple. He must have gone there to thank God that he was well again. Jesus said to him: "You are well again. Do not sin any more, or something worse may happen to you."

Now the man knew it was Jesus who had cured him. He went and told the leaders: "It was Jesus who made me well."

Because Jesus had done these things on a Sabbath day, the leaders of the people thought He had disobeyed God's law, and they were angry with Jesus.

But Jesus said to them: "My Father works all the time, and so do I." That made the leaders still more angry, because He called God His own Father and made Himself God.

John 5:1-18

Jesus and His First Disciples

Peter's Draft of Fishes

One bright morning Jesus was teaching near the Sea of Galilee. So many people crowded around Him that it was hard for Him to speak.

Some fishermen had brought their boats close to shore and had left them while they washed their nets. Jesus stepped into one of the boats, which belonged to Simon Peter, and asked him to push it out a little from the land. Jesus sat down in the boat and taught the people.

After the sermon, Jesus said to Simon: "Row out to the deep water, and let down your nets for a catch of fish." Simon answered: "Master, we worked all night and did not catch anything. But because You say so, I will let down the nets."

When the fishermen let down the nets into the water, they caught so many fish that the nets began to tear. They waved to their partners in the other boat to come and help them pull up the nets.

They now filled both boats so full of fish that the boats began to sink.

When Simon Peter saw the miracle, he fell down at Jesus' knees and said: "Go away from me, for I am a sinful man, O Lord."

The miracle showed that Jesus is the almighty Son of God, and Peter felt that he was too sinful to be near Jesus. But Jesus said to Peter: "Do not be afraid any more. From now on you will catch men alive."

Jesus meant that Peter and his partners would be missionaries who would tell many people of the Savior and His love. So when they had brought the boats to land, they left everything behind and followed Jesus.

Luke 5:1-11

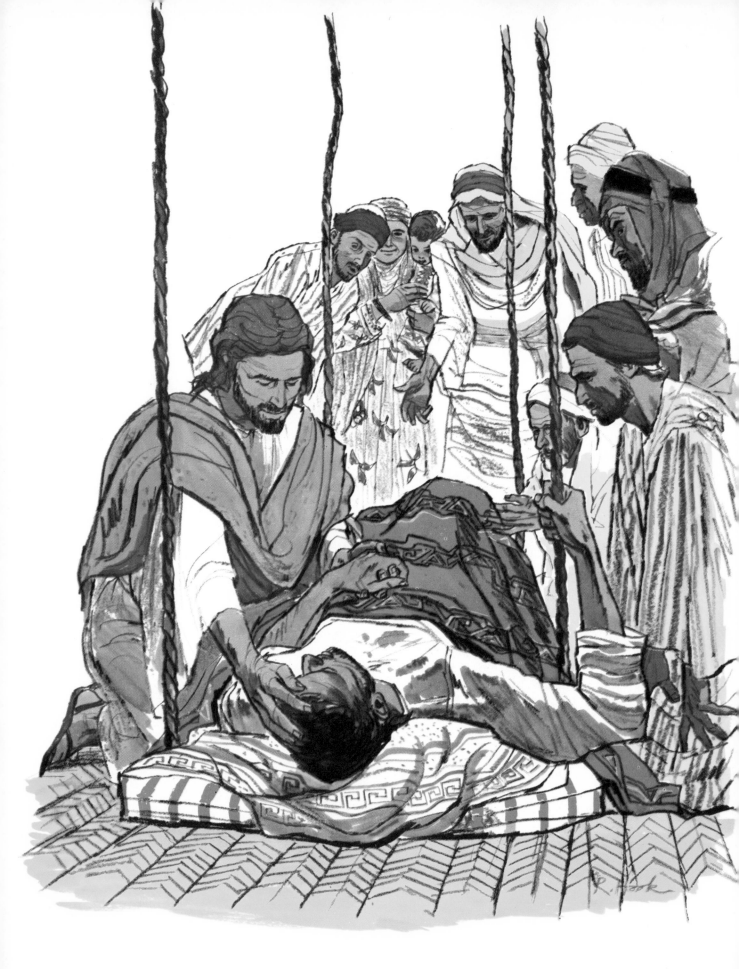

Jesus Healing the Man Sick of the Palsy

The Man Sick of the Palsy

In a city called Capernaum there lived a very sick man. He could not move and he had great pain. So he had to lie helpless in bed.

One day some friends told him that Jesus was in Capernaum. The sick man believed that Jesus could help him. He wanted to go to Jesus.

So his friends laid him on a pallet and carried him to the house where Jesus was. But when they got there, they found the house so crowded with people that they could not get in.

The friends knew what to do. They carried the sick man up an outside stairway to the roof. They made a hole in the roof, tied ropes to the pallet, and let the man down through the hole into the house.

Now the man was right in front of Jesus. Jesus knew he was sorry that he had sinned, so He said to him: "Your sins are forgiven."

The man was glad that his sins were forgiven. But Jesus took away his sickness, too. He said: "Get up, take your pallet, and go to your house."

As soon as Jesus had said this, the man got up. He picked up his pallet and went home. He was thankful and happy, for Jesus had forgiven his sins and had also made him well.

Mark 2:1-12

Jesus and Matthew

The Calling of Matthew

In the land where Jesus lived there were some men who were called publicans. The publicans gathered tax money for the king.

Often they took more money than was right. In this way they stole and made themselves rich. That is why people hated them and would have nothing to do with them.

A publican named Matthew gathered tax money by the side of a road near Capernaum. One day Jesus went along the same road.

When Jesus came to Matthew, He stopped and said to him: "Follow Me." Jesus wanted Matthew to come with Him and be one of His disciples. Matthew got up and followed Jesus.

Soon after this, Matthew invited Jesus and His disciples to a dinner at his house. Matthew also invited some of his friends who were publicans. A number of people who were not invited also came.

Some men called Pharisees were outside on the street in front of Matthew's house. These men were very proud. They hated publicans and thought themselves better than other people.

The Pharisees were displeased to see Jesus go to Matthew's house and eat dinner with sinful people. They thought that Jesus should have nothing to do with sinners.

After the dinner the Pharisees asked the disciples: "Why does your Master eat and drink with publicans and sinners?"

Jesus heard this. He said to the Pharisees: "People who are well do not need a doctor, only they who are sick need him. I have not come to help holy people, but I have come to help sinners."

With these words Jesus meant to say to the Pharisees: "You think you are good and do not need Me. These publicans know they are sinners, and I have come to save them so that they will go to heaven."

Jesus is the Friend of sinners.

Matthew 9:9-13; Mark 2:14-17; Luke 5:27-32

Jesus Talking to People About Their Heavenly Father

God's Care for His Children

Jesus taught His disciples many lessons that will also help us live as children of God. One of these lessons is that God, our heavenly Father, cares for us. And for that reason we should not worry.

He said: "Are not two sparrows sold for a penny? And one of them will not fall on the ground and die unless your Father allows it to die. But even the hairs of your head have all been counted.

"For that reason you are not to be afraid. You are worth more than many sparrows, and God will take care of you."

Another time Jesus said: "Do not worry about your life and what you will eat and drink. Do not worry about your body, what you will wear.

"Look at the birds. They do not sow or reap or store up food in barns, and your heavenly Father feeds them. Are you not worth more than the birds?"

Jesus said: "Who of you can make his life last one bit longer by worrying? Look at the lilies of the field, and watch how they grow. They do not work. They do not spin.

"But I say to you that Solomon in all his fine clothes was not dressed like one of these lilies. If God makes the lilies so pretty, He will surely take care of you.

"So do not worry and say, 'What shall we eat? What shall we drink? What shall we wear?' For people who do not believe in God worry about all these things.

"Your heavenly Father knows that you need them. See that you keep on trusting in God and serving Him, and He will give you everything you need."

Matthew 6:24-34; 10:29-31

The Roman Centurion with His Sick Servant

The Centurion of Capernaum

At the time of Jesus the land of Israel was ruled by the Romans, who were a Gentile people. There were Roman soldiers in all the main cities.

At Capernaum there lived a Roman centurion. A centurion was a captain over a hundred soldiers.

The centurion had a servant who was very dear to him, but this servant was sick with a very painful disease called palsy. He was not expected to live.

The centurion felt sorry for his sick servant. He heard about Jesus and His wonderful works. He wondered whether Jesus would help him even though he was a Gentile.

He did not dare to go to Jesus himself, so he sent some of the leaders of the people to ask Jesus to heal his servant.

These leaders went to Jesus and begged Him to come and make the centurion's servant well. They told Jesus that the centurion deserved to be helped because he loved the people and had built a church for them.

At once Jesus said: "I will go and heal him," and He went with them. But when He was not far from the house, the centurion sent some other friends to Jesus, saying: "Lord, I am not worthy that Thou shouldest enter under my roof. Just speak the word, and my servant shall be healed."

The centurion showed strong faith in Jesus. He did not think that he was good enough to have the Lord Jesus in his house.

He also said: "I am only a man, but when I say to one soldier, 'Go,' he goes; and to another, 'Come,' he comes." He meant to say that if Jesus would only say, "Go," to the sickness, it would surely have to go away, because Jesus is God.

When Jesus heard this, He was surprised at the strong faith of this Gentile. He said: "I have not found so great faith, no, not in Israel."

Later the men who were sent returned to the centurion's house and they found that the servant had become completely well that very same hour.

Luke 7:1-10

Jesus Stills the Storm

The Stilling of the Storm

Jesus was near the Sea of Galilee. All day He was busy teaching a large crowd of people and healing those who were sick. In the evening He sent the people away.

But He and His disciples got into a boat and started across the sea. Jesus lay down in the back part of the boat and fell asleep. He was very tired.

Soon a storm came up. Black clouds covered the sky. The wind blew harder and harder. High waves splashed water into the ship. The disciples were afraid. They thought they would surely drown. They came to Jesus and cried: "Lord, save us!"

Jesus awoke, and He said to them: "Why are you afraid?" Then He stood up and spoke to the wind. He said: "Peace, be still!"

As soon as Jesus had said this, the storm was over, and all was very quiet.

Why had the disciples been afraid? They had forgotten that Jesus is the almighty Son of God, that He loves His children dearly, and will help them in every trouble.

Matthew 8:23-27; Mark 4:36-41; Luke 8:22-25

Jesus Makes the Girl Alive Again

The Raising of Jairus' Daughter

In the city of Capernaum there lived a man named Jairus with his wife and daughter. The daughter was twelve years old. One day she became sick. She grew worse all the time. She was dying.

Jesus was in Capernaum, and Jairus hurried to Him. As soon as he met Jesus, he knelt down and prayed: "My daughter is very sick. Come and lay your hands on her to heal her, then she will live."

Together they started on their way. But before they had gone far, a man came from Jairus' house and said to him, "Your daughter is dead. There is no need to trouble the Master anymore."

But Jesus said to Jairus: "Do not be afraid, only believe."

When they came to the house, they found it filled with people.

Women were crying and weeping, and men were playing funeral music. Jesus said to them: "Why do you make all this noise? The girl is not dead; she is asleep."

The people thought it was foolish to say the girl was asleep. They knew she was dead. So they laughed at Jesus. Jesus told them all to leave the house.

He led the father and the mother into the room where their dead daughter lay. He took her by the hand and said: "Little girl, I say to you: Arise!"

At once the girl got up. Jesus had made the girl alive again.

Soon the story of this miracle spread through all the land.

Matthew 9:18-26; Mark 5:22-43; Luke 8:41-56

Jesus Feeds Many People

Feeding of the Five Thousand

Jesus wanted to rest, so He took His disciples to a lonely place across the Sea of Galilee. But the people saw where they were going, and followed them.

Jesus felt sorry for the people. He taught them and healed the sick. Then He went up the side of a hill and sat down with His disciples.

Soon they could see thousands of people coming up to them. Jesus said to Philip: "Where shall we buy bread to feed so many people?"

Jesus wanted to see if Philip would trust in Him to feed the people. But Philip answered: "If we had money for many loaves of bread, there would not be enough to give each one just a little."

During the rest of the day, Jesus taught the people. In the evening the disciples began to worry. They came to Jesus and asked Him to send the people away.

But Jesus wanted to see if the disciples would trust in Him to feed the people. He said: "You give them food to eat." They were surprised, for they had no food. They asked: "Shall we go and buy bread for them to eat?"

Now the time had come for Jesus to help. He asked: "How many loaves do you have?" Andrew said: "There is a boy who has five barley loaves and two small fishes."

Jesus said: "Tell the people to sit down." There were five thousand men, besides women and children, in the crowd.

When they were seated, Jesus took the five loaves and the two fishes. He looked up to heaven and thanked God. He blessed the loaves and the fishes. He gave the food to the disciples, and the disciples gave it to the people. There was enough for all of them.

When all had eaten and were satisfied, Jesus said to His disciples: "Gather up the pieces so that nothing will be wasted." The disciples filled twelve baskets full of food.

But the people who saw the miracle Jesus had done said: "This is that Prophet whom God promised to send."

Mark 6:30-44; John 6:1-14

"Lord, Save Me!"

Jesus Walks on the Water

Some of the people who saw the wonderful way in which Jesus had fed them wanted to make Him their King. They thought He would always feed them and use His great power to drive their enemies away.

But this did not please Jesus, because He had come to be the heavenly King and Savior of all people. So Jesus told His disciples to get into their boat and row across to the other side of the Sea of Galilee.

After teaching the crowds God's Word He sent them away and went up into the mountain alone. He wanted to talk to His heavenly Father in prayer.

That night, as the disciples were crossing the sea, a big storm came up. Jesus allowed the storm to come in order to teach His disciples another lesson.

The wind blew hard, and the disciples rowed with all their might, but they seemed to get nowhere because the wind was against them.

About three o'clock that morning the disciples saw something moving on the water. It was coming toward their boat. At first the disciples thought it was a ghost and cried out in fear.

But it was Jesus, who was coming to His disciples in this wonderful way. He was walking on the water just as we walk on land.

"Be of good cheer; it is I; be not afraid," called Jesus. Hearing these words, Peter said: "Lord, if it is You, tell me to come to You on the water." Jesus said: "Come." So Peter began to walk toward Jesus on the water.

But before Peter reached Jesus, he saw a big wave coming toward him, and he became afraid. At once he began to sink and cried out: "Lord, save me!"

Quickly Jesus stretched out His hand, caught Peter, and said to him: "How little you trust Me! Why did you doubt?"

As Jesus and Peter stepped into the boat the winds stopped. Those who were in the boat were very much surprised at the wonderful power of Jesus.

They worshiped Him and said: "You certainly are the Son of God!" They had learned their lesson.

Matthew 14:22-33; Mark 6:47-52; John 6:16-21

The Good Samaritan

The Good Samaritan

"Who is my neighbor?" a lawyer once asked Jesus. To answer the question, Jesus told this story.

A certain man was going from Jerusalem to Jericho. On the way some robbers saw him. They stopped him, took his money, tore off his clothing, and beat him until he was nearly dead.

Then they ran away, leaving the poor man on the roadside.

After a while a priest happened to come that way. He saw the wounded man, but did not stop to help him. He hurried by on the other side of the road.

Soon another man came along. This man was a Levite. He worked in the Temple and was supposed to be a very holy person. The Levite, too, saw the wounded man, but did not help him. Like the priest, he passed by on the other side of the road.

At last a Samaritan came the same way. He looked at the wounded man and saw that he was one of the Jewish people. He knew that the Samaritans and the Jewish people were not friends. Just the same he went to the man on the roadside and helped him. He cleaned his wounds and put bandages on them. Then he put the man on his donkey and brought him to an inn. There he took care of him.

The next morning the Samaritan had to travel farther. Before he went away, he gave some money to the innkeeper and said: "Take care of the man. If more money is needed, I will give it to you when I come again."

This is the story that Jesus told. After the story He said to the lawyer: "Which of the three do you think was a neighbor to the man who was robbed?"

The lawyer answered: "The one who was kind to him."

Then Jesus said: "That is right; now go and do as the Samaritan did."

Jesus wants us to be kind to everyone.

Luke 10:25-37

"Martha, You Are Troubled About Many Things"

Mary and Martha

Jesus often went up to Jerusalem to teach and to be at the services in the Temple. On His journeys He liked to stay in the quiet little town of Bethany, which was near Jerusalem.

Here lived some good friends of Jesus. They were the sisters Mary and Martha and their brother Lazarus.

One day Jesus came to Bethany, and Martha invited Him to her house. Jesus was pleased to come, and the sisters knew it was a great honor to have Jesus as their Guest.

When Jesus came to their house, He sat down to teach. Mary sat down at the feet of Jesus and listened closely to every word He spoke. Nothing gave her so much joy as to listen to Jesus teaching the Word of God.

While Mary sat there listening, Martha was running back and forth, very much excited about the meal. She loved Jesus just as Mary did, and she thought the best way to honor the Lord was to make a good supper for Him.

Martha was displeased because Mary did not come and help her. She went to Jesus and said: "Lord, do You not care that my sister is leaving all the work to me? Tell her to come and help me."

Jesus looked at Martha in His friendly way and said: "Martha, Martha, you are worried and troubled about many things. But one thing is needful. Mary has chosen the good part which shall not be taken away from her."

The best thing for all of us is first to hear the Word of Jesus and then do our work.

Luke 10:38-42

"He Put His Arms Around Him"

The Prodigal Son

One day some people were surprised to see Jesus talking with sinners. To show that He is ready to forgive sinners who are sorry for their sins, Jesus told this story.

There was a man who had two sons. One day the younger son said to his father: "Give me my share of the money that you are going to leave us someday." So the father gave the young man all that he had been saving for him.

A few days afterward the young man gathered all that was his and went far away from home. There he wasted his money in sinful pleasures, and soon it was all gone.

Then a great famine came into the land, and the young man had nothing to eat. Now he had to work for his living, but work was hard to find.

At last a man living there sent him out on his field to take care of his pigs. The young man was so hungry that he wished to eat the food that was given to the pigs.

One day he began to think how foolish he had been. He said to himself, "At home my father's servants have plenty to eat, while I am dying of hunger. I will go to my father and say, 'Father, I have sinned. I am not worthy to be called your son. Let me be one of your servants.'"

At once the young man started on his way home. When he was still far down the road, his father saw him coming and pitied him. He ran out to meet him. He put his arms around him and kissed him.

The son said: "Father, I have sinned. I am not worthy to be called your son."

But the father said to his servants: "Bring the best robe, and put it on him. Put a ring on his hand and shoes on his feet. Make a feast, and let us eat and be merry. For my son was dead and is alive again; he was lost and is found."

Like the father in the story, God is ready and glad to receive anyone who is sorry for his sins and turns back to Him.

Luke 15:1-2, 11-32

Mary and Martha Are Happy that Their Brother
Lazarus Is Alive Again

The Raising of Lazarus

Mary and Martha were good friends of Jesus. They lived in the little town of Bethany. They had a brother named Lazarus. One day Lazarus became very sick. The sisters thought of their Friend Jesus right away and sent someone to Him with the message, "Lord, He whom You love is sick."

When Jesus heard the news, He said: "This sickness is not to end in death, but it is to glorify the Son of God." Now, Jesus loved Mary and Martha and Lazarus very much, but still He stayed two more days in the place where He was.

After that Jesus said to His disciples: "Our friend Lazarus is sleeping; but I am going to wake him out of his sleep."

At first they thought that Lazarus was sleeping as we sleep at night and that he would soon wake up. Then Jesus told them plainly: "Lazarus is dead."

When Jesus came to Bethany, Lazarus had been in the grave four days already. Martha said: "Lord, if You had been here, my brother would not have died."

Then Jesus said: "Your brother will rise again." Martha said: "I know he will rise again on the Last Day."

Jesus said: "I am the Resurrection and the Life; he that believeth in Me, though he were dead, yet shall he live." Jesus now asked Martha: "Do you believe this?"

Martha answered: "Yes, Lord, I believe that You are the Christ, the Son of God."

When also Mary had come out to meet Jesus, they went to the grave of Lazarus. Many people had come to comfort Mary and Martha. All of them were weeping. Mary said: "Lord, if You had been here, my brother would not have died." At the grave even Jesus wept.

The grave was like a cave, and a big stone had been put in front of the opening. Jesus said to the men: "Take away the stone." Then He looked up to heaven and prayed aloud.

After that He said with a loud voice: "Lazarus, come out!" And Lazarus, who had been dead four days, came out of the grave and was alive again.

Lazarus was wrapped from head to foot in graveclothes. Jesus said to the people: "Unwrap him, and let him go."

When the people saw this great miracle, many of them believed that Jesus surely must be the Son of God.

John 11:1-46

Only One of the Lepers Came to Thank Jesus

The Ten Lepers

Jesus was going into a little town when ten men met Him. These men had a very bad sickness called leprosy.

Lepers were not allowed to live in towns or to come near to other people because of their dreadful sickness. So the ten men stood there by themselves, away from the people.

But they cried out as loudly as they could: "Jesus, Master, help us!" These men believed that Jesus could make them well, just as He had made many other sick persons well.

Jesus saw the ten sick men standing there. He also heard them begging for help. But He did not make them well at once. "Go and show yourselves to the priest," He said.

If lepers got over their sickness, the priests were to look at them. The priests were to say whether they were cured and could live with other people again.

The lepers obeyed the word of Jesus, even though He did not make them well at once. They started on the road to Jerusalem to show themselves to the priest in the Temple.

All at once, as they were walking along, they found that the sickness had left them. Jesus had answered their prayer and made them well.

One of the ten men turned back at once and praised God with a loud voice. He came to Jesus and fell down at the feet of Jesus and thanked Him. This man was a Samaritan.

Jesus looked at the Samaritan lying there on the ground before Him. "Were not ten cured?" He asked. "Where are the nine others? This Samaritan is the only one who has come back to thank God."

Jesus said to him: "Arise, go on your way. Because you believed My Word, you were made well."

Luke 17:11-19

Jesus and the Children

Jesus Blesses Little Children

One day, while Jesus was teaching a crowd of people, some mothers brought their babies and little children to Him.

They wanted Jesus to lay His hands on them and bless them as God's dear children.

The disciples spoke rudely to the mothers who had brought their children, and tried to send them away. They thought Jesus was too busy or too tired to be bothered with children.

They did not believe that Jesus could do anything for babies and children who were too young to understand His teaching.

But when Jesus saw this, He was very much displeased. He said to His disciples:

"Let the little children come to Me. Do not stop them, for of such is the kingdom of God."

Jesus even said that if grown-up people did not believe in Him as little children do, they could not come into heaven.

Jesus welcomed the little babies and children and showed everyone how much He loved them. He took them up in His arms and held them close to Him.

He laid His hands on them, spoke kindly to them, and gave them His love.

The mothers and the children were very happy when they went back to their homes. They knew that Jesus is the Friend of little children.

Mark 10:13-16

The Rich Young Ruler

The Rich Young Ruler

Jesus and His disciples were going to Jerusalem. On the way a young man came running to them. This young man was a ruler. He had charge of the synagog, the house of worship, and he was rich.

He knelt down at the feet of Jesus and said: "Good Master, what must I do to get to heaven?"

Jesus said: "Keep the commandments."

"Which commandments must I keep?" asked the young man.

Jesus answered: "You know the commandments: Thou shalt not kill; Thou shalt not commit adultery; Thou shalt not steal; Thou shalt not bear false witness; Honor thy father and thy mother; Thou shalt love thy neighbor as thyself."

The young man was pleased when he heard this. He said: "I have kept all of these ever since I was a small child. Is there anything else I must do?"

Jesus loved the young man and felt sorry for him. He saw that money was dearer to him than God.

So Jesus said: "To be perfect there is one more thing that you must do. Sell all you have, and give the money to the poor. Then come and follow Me."

When the young man heard this, he walked away sad, for he loved his money and did not want to give it away.

As Jesus watched him go, He said: "How hard it is for those who trust in riches to enter the kingdom of God!"

As long as we love anything more than Jesus, we cannot go to heaven.

Matthew 19:16-30; Mark 10:17-31; Luke 18:18-30

Jesus Touches the Eyes of Blind Bartimaeus

Blind Bartimaeus

It was springtime, and Jesus and His disciples were walking toward Jerusalem. A large crowd of people followed them. To get to Jerusalem they had to pass through the city of Jericho.

Outside this city a poor blind man sat by the roadside, begging for money. His name was Bartimaeus. As he sat there, he heard the sound of many people passing by, and he asked why the crowd was on the road. Someone told him, "Jesus of Nazareth is passing by."

Bartimaeus had heard of Jesus before. Everywhere people were talking about him, about His preaching and miracles. Bartimaeus believed that Jesus is the Son of God and that He has the power to heal the eyes of the blind and make them see.

So he began to cry out: "Jesus, Thou Son of David, have mercy on me!"

He called so loudly that he annoyed some of the people. They told him to keep still. But Bartimaeus did not keep still. He cried out louder than before, saying over and over: "Son of David, have mercy on me!"

Jesus heard the prayer of the blind man, and He wished to help him. He stopped and told the people to bring the blind man to Him.

Then someone hurried over to where Bartimaeus was sitting and said: "Jesus is calling you."

As soon as Bartimaeus heard this, he got up and went to Jesus. Jesus asked him: "What do you want Me to do to you?"

Bartimaeus answered: "Lord, I would like to receive my sight."

Jesus felt sorry for the poor blind man. He touched his eyes and said: "Because you believe in Me, receive your sight."

When Jesus had said this, Bartimaeus could see. How happy he was! He joined the crowd following Jesus and praised and thanked God for His goodness.

All the other people who saw the miracle also praised God.

Matthew 20:29-34; Mark 10:46-52; Luke 18:35-43

Zacchaeus in the Tree

Zacchaeus

In Jericho there lived a man whose name was Zacchaeus. He was a rich publican. You may remember that publicans were taxgatherers and that they were much disliked by the people.

Often they collected more than was right and kept the extra money. That is why the people hated them and called them great sinners.

One day Jesus was passing through Jericho. When Zacchaeus heard that Jesus was in his city, he wanted very much to see Him.

So he hurried out and joined the crowd that was following Jesus; however, when Zacchaeus came to the place where Jesus was, he could not see Him. The trouble was that Zacchaeus was a short man, and he could not see over the heads of the crowd around Jesus.

But Zacchaeus had an idea that would help him. He ran ahead of the crowd and climbed up a tree. There he waited for Jesus to pass by. When Jesus came to the tree, He stopped and looked at Zacchaeus.

He said: "Zacchaeus, come down quickly, for I must stay at your house a while today."

Zacchaeus was glad when he heard this. He climbed down quickly and took Jesus to his house.

Some of the people in the crowd were displeased when they saw it. They thought it was wrong for Jesus to visit with a great sinner such as Zacchaeus.

They said: "Jesus has gone to be the guest of a man who is a sinner."

Jesus paid no attention to what the people said. He went with Zacchaeus to his house. There Zacchaeus told Him that he was sorry for his sins.

He said: "Lord, half of all I have I will give to the poor. And if I have cheated anyone, I will pay back four times as much as I took."

Jesus was pleased when He heard this. He said: "Today salvation has come to this house; for the Son of Man is come to seek and to save that which is lost."

Luke 19:1-10

Mary Dried the Feet of Jesus with Her Hair

Mary Anoints Jesus

A few days before Jesus suffered and died, He went with His disciples to Bethany, the home of Mary and Martha.

Another friend of Jesus, Simon the leper, lived there, too. Simon prepared a supper for Jesus and His disciples, and invited Mary, Martha, and Lazarus, their brother.

While they were eating, Mary went to Jesus with a box of very fine and costly perfume. She broke the box open and poured the perfume on Jesus' head and feet. Then she bent low and dried His feet with her hair. She did this because she loved Jesus.

The disciples saw what Mary had done and were displeased. They thought the perfume had been wasted.

One of the disciples, whose name was Judas, said: "Why was the perfume not sold and the money given to the poor?"

But Jesus was pleased with the thing Mary had done. He said: "Let this woman alone. She has done a good work for Me. You will have the poor with you always, but you will not have Me always."

Jesus also said: "Wherever the Word of God is preached in all the world, people will remember Mary and speak of the good thing she has done."

Matthew 26:6-13; John 12:1-8

Jesus Rides into Jerusalem

Jesus Rides to Jerusalem

It was festival time in the land where Jesus lived. The roads were crowded with happy people. They sang as they walked along. They were going to Jerusalem for the Feast of the Passover.

Jesus, too, was on His way to Jerusalem. The time was near for Him to suffer and die to save the world from sin.

When Jesus came near a small town, He called two of His disciples and said: "Go into the village. There you will find a colt and its mother. Untie them, and bring them to Me."

Jesus also said: "If anyone asks you why you are taking the animals, say, 'The Lord needs them'; then the owners will let you have them."

The disciples went and found the animals. While they were untying them, the owners came and said: "Why are you doing this?" The disciples answered, "The Lord needs them." Then the owners let the disciples take the animals.

The disciples came back to Jesus and laid their coats on the colt to make a saddle. Next they set Jesus on the colt, and He began His ride to Jerusalem as a King.

The people in Jerusalem heard that Jesus was coming as their King. So large crowds came out to meet Him. Some of the people spread their coats on the road in front of Jesus. Others cut branches from palm trees and laid them on the road.

The crowds that went before Jesus and those that followed after Him praised Him joyfully. They sang: "Hosanna to the Son of David! Blessed is He that cometh in the name of the Lord! Hosanna in the highest!"

Jesus rode into the city and went to the Temple. There some children came and praised Him. They sang "Hosanna to the Son of David!"

Matthew 21:1-9

"There Was a Man Who Had Two Sons"

The Parable of the Two Sons

One day when Jesus visited the Temple, the chief priests and elders came to Him. These church leaders were enemies of Jesus. They did not believe that Jesus was the Son of God.

They liked to pretend that they loved God very much. They prayed in the street and even told God how good they were. But they did not really love God. They were not sorry for their sins, and they did not really obey God.

When these wicked men came to Jesus, He told them this story. He said: "There was a man who had two sons. He went to the first son and said, 'Son, go and work in my vineyard today.' But the son answered, 'I will not go.'

"A little later he was sorry for his wickedness, and so he obeyed his father and went to work in the vineyard. The father said to the second son, 'Son, go and work in the vineyard today.' This second son said, 'I will go, sir.' But he did not go."

Jesus asked the church leaders: "Which of the two sons did the will of his father?" They answered: "The first son." Then Jesus said to them: "It is true that thieves and sinful women will be saved. But you will not.

"The sinners were sorry for their sins. They listened to the preaching of John and changed their ways. But you did not believe John. You are not sorry for your sins, and you do not believe in Me. You will be lost."

Matthew 21:28-32

Jesus Was Pleased with the Poor Widow

The Widow's Mites

On one of His visits to the Temple, Jesus sat down near the place where thirteen offering boxes stood. Into these boxes the people put money for the upkeep of the Temple.

For some time Jesus watched the people dropping money into the boxes. He saw the rich people put large sums of money into them. He saw others give smaller sums.

While Jesus was sitting there watching, a poor widow woman passed by. She dropped two mites, or little pieces of copper money, worth less than a penny, into one of the boxes. It was the last of her money, but she gave it because she loved God and was thankful.

Jesus was pleased with the poor widow, who was so thankful to God that she gave the last of her money. He called His disciples to Him and said: "This poor widow has given more than all the other people together. For the others still had plenty of money left after they gave their offerings. But this woman gave all her money."

This widow had no money left for food and for the other things she needed. She depended on God, the heavenly Father, to give her food and clothing and whatever else she needed.

Mark 12:41-44; Luke 21:1-4

"Jesus Took Some Bread, and Gave Thanks to His
Heavenly Father"

The Lord's Supper

The Tuesday before Jesus died, His enemies held a meeting to plan how they might take Him and kill Him.

At that time the devil entered the heart of Judas, one of the twelve disciples of Jesus, and made Judas willing to betray Jesus. Judas went to the enemies of Jesus and promised to help them capture Jesus if they would give him thirty pieces of silver.

On Thursday evening Jesus and His disciples were in a large upstairs room. Jesus had just washed their feet and they were about to have a last supper together. After they had taken their places at the table Jesus said: "One of you will betray Me."

The disciples were sad when they heard this, and one after another asked: "Lord, is it I?" Even Judas dared to ask: "Master, is it I?"

Jesus answered, "Yes," and told Judas to go quickly and do his wicked deed. Judas left in a hurry and it was night.

As the rest were eating, Jesus took some bread, gave thanks to His heavenly Father, and broke it. Then He gave it to His disciples and said: "Take, eat; this is My body, which is given for you. This do in remembrance of Me."

In the same way He took a cup of wine, and after giving thanks, He gave it to them, saying: "Take, drink of it, all of you; this cup is the new testament in My blood, which is shed for you for the forgiveness of sins. This do, as often as you drink it, in remembrance of Me."

Matthew 26:14-29; Luke 22:19-20

Jesus Praying to His Heavenly Father for Strength

Jesus in Gethsemane

The time had come for Jesus to suffer and die. The evening before He died, He took His disciples into a garden, not far from Jerusalem, called Gethsemane. Jesus left most of the disciples near the gate. He said: "Stay here while I go and pray."

He took Peter, James, and John farther into the garden. There He began to be sorrowful and troubled in His heart, for His suffering for the sins of all people had begun. He said to the three disciples: "Stay here; watch and pray with Me."

Then Jesus went away by Himself and prayed. After the prayer He came back to His disciples and found them asleep. He did this three times.

The third time there was a noise at the garden gate. The disciple named Judas was coming with a crowd of soldiers and other men. They carried lights and swords.

They were coming to take Jesus and put Him to death. When they were near, Judas stepped out of the crowd. He said to Jesus: "Hail, Master," and kissed Him.

He did this to show the soldiers whom to capture and lead away. The soldiers crowded around Jesus, took hold of Him, and tied Him.

Peter wanted to fight for Jesus. He drew his sword and struck a man, cutting off his ear. Jesus told Peter to put his sword away, and healed the man's ear. After that the enemies led Jesus away.

The disciples saw this and became afraid. They all ran away, leaving Jesus alone with His enemies.

Matthew 26:30-57; John 18:1-13

145

Jesus and Pontius Pilate

Christ Before Pilate

The people who wanted to put Jesus to death brought Him to Pilate, the governor. Pilate was the only one who had the right to have someone put to death. He asked: "What wrong has this Man done?"

Jesus had done nothing wrong. So the people made up lies. They said: "He has caused trouble in the land. He has turned the people against the king. He says He is king."

Pilate went to Jesus and said: "Are You the king of the Jews?"

Jesus answered: "My kingdom is not of this world."

Then Pilate asked: "Are You a king, then?"

"Yes," Jesus said, "I am a King."

Jesus meant to say: I am not a king like other kings, but a King who rules with the Word of God.

Pilate turned to the people and said: "I find no fault in this Man."

But the people shouted: "Crucify Him!"

Then Pilate had his soldiers whip Jesus. They whipped Him and put an old purple coat on Him. They also made a crown of thorns and put it on Jesus.

They bowed before Him to make fun of Him because He had said He was a King. They spit on Jesus and hit Him on the head.

How pitiful Jesus looked! Pilate brought Him before the people. He thought they would feel sorry for Him. But they did not feel sorry at all. They cried: "Crucify Him! Crucify Him!"

Pilate saw that the people were angry, and he was afraid of them. So he let them have their way. He told his soldiers to nail Jesus to a cross and put Him to death.

He washed his hands before the people and said: "I do not want the blame for killing this good Man."

Then they led Jesus away to crucify Him.

Matthew 27:1-31; Mark 15:1-19; Luke 23:1-25;
John 18:28 — 19:16

Jesus Being Crucified

The Death and Burial of Jesus

Outside the city of Jerusalem was a place called Calvary. Jesus was led there by the soldiers. Jesus carried His cross part of the way. Then the soldiers made a man named Simon carry it the rest of the way. Other people cried for Jesus. They did not know that Jesus was doing this for them.

The enemies of Jesus crucified Him. They nailed His hands and feet to the cross. Jesus' cross was put up between two others, on which robbers were crucified. Soldiers took Jesus' clothes. His enemies called Him names and mocked Him. Even the robbers on the cross mocked Him.

This added to Jesus' suffering. For about six hours Jesus hung on the cross. He was suffering and dying to pay for the sins of the whole world.

Jesus spoke seven times from the cross. These words tell us how He felt and what was happening. First, Jesus prayed for His enemies who put Him on the cross.

He said: "Father, forgive them, for they know not what they do." Then one of the robbers was sorry for his sins and prayed to Jesus. He said: "Remember me when You come into Your kingdom." Jesus said to him: "Today you will be with Me in heaven."

Jesus looked down from the cross and saw His mother, Mary, and His disciple John. He said to Mary: "John will take care of you as a son." To John He said: "See, your mother!" From that time John took care of Mary in his own house.

As Jesus suffered on the cross, darkness came over the land. Jesus cried: "My God, My God, why have You forsaken Me?"

Then He said: "I am thirsty." His enemies gave Him vinegar to drink. Soon after that Jesus knew that His work was done. He had paid the price of sin.

He shouted in victory: "It is finished!" His last words were, "Father, into Your hands I give My spirit."

Then He bowed His head and died. The sins of all people were paid for because Jesus paid the price by His holy suffering and death on the cross.

Late in the afternoon some of Jesus' friends asked Pilate for the body of the Lord. They took down the body and laid it in a grave.

They closed the door of the grave with a large stone. Some women who loved Jesus watched where they buried Him.

Matthew 27:31-60; Mark 15:20-47; Luke 23:26-56; John 19:16-42

Now Mary Knew Jesus. She Cried, "Master!"

The Resurrection of Jesus

It was the second morning after Jesus had died on the cross. Soldiers were guarding the grave. Suddenly the earth shook. A great light shone down from heaven.

An angel came and rolled away the stone from the door of the grave. The soldiers became afraid. They fell to the ground as if they were dead.

The grave was empty! Jesus was alive again! The soldiers got up and ran into the city. They told Jesus' enemies everything that had happened.

Then the enemies gave money to the soldiers. They told them to say that they had been sleeping and that the disciples had taken the body of Jesus away.

Very early the same morning some of the women who believed in Jesus came out to the grave. They saw that the grave was open. What had happened? Jesus was not there.

Then the angel gave them this message:

"I know that you are looking for Jesus of Nazareth, who was crucified. He is not here, for He is risen, as He said. Come, see the place where the Lord lay. And go quickly and tell His disciples, 'He is risen from the dead.'" At once the women hurried to bring the message to the disciples.

That same morning Jesus showed Himself alive first to Mary Magdalene. Mary was crying when Jesus suddenly stood near her and spoke to her. Mary thought the man in charge of the garden was speaking.

"Sir," she said, "if you have taken Him away, tell me where you have laid Him." "Mary!" said Jesus. Now Mary knew Jesus.

She cried: "Master!" Jesus said to her: "Go and tell My disciples that I am alive again and that soon I will go to My Father in heaven."

Mary was very happy on that Easter Day. She ran to the disciples and gave them the message that Jesus was alive.

Matthew 27:57 — 28:15; Luke 24:1-12

They Knew It Was Jesus

The Emmaus Disciples

On the afternoon of the first Easter Day two disciples left Jerusalem. They walked to the little town of Emmaus. They talked, too, of all the things that had happened to Jesus.

A stranger joined them and listened. It was Jesus Himself! But Jesus did not want the disciples to know Him at once, and so they did not know Him.

Jesus said: "What are you talking about, and why are you sad?" The disciples answered: "Are you a stranger in Jerusalem? Have you not heard of the things which have happened there in these days?" "What things?" Jesus asked.

They began to tell Him how the enemies of Jesus had put Him to death on the cross.

They said: "We had hoped He would be our Savior. But He has been dead three days already. Some of the women told us that they went to the grave early this morning. They did not find the body of Jesus there.

"They saw angels instead. The angels told them, 'Jesus is alive.' Some of the disciples went to the grave, and found it empty. But they did not see Jesus alive! That is why we are sad."

"Oh, how foolish you are," said the Stranger. "You should believe what the Bible says. God's Word long ago said the Savior must die for sinners."

Then He explained to them all the sayings in the Bible which showed that Jesus had to suffer and die to be the Savior. The disciples listened. How happy they were that this Stranger helped them understand God's Word!

When they came to the village, Jesus acted as though He would go farther. But the disciples did not want Him to leave them. They said: "Stay with us, for it is evening."

Jesus was willing to stay with them. As they sat down to eat, Jesus took bread and prayed and gave it to them.

Suddenly the disciples' eyes were opened, and they knew it was Jesus. As soon as they knew Him, Jesus was gone.

Luke 24:13-32

Thomas Said, "My Lord and My God!"

Thomas

On the evening of Easter Sunday the disciples of Jesus were together in a room. They locked all the doors, for they were afraid of the enemies of Jesus who had crucified their Lord.

They talked about how Jesus died and rose again. All of the disciples were there except Thomas.

Suddenly Jesus stood among them. "Peace be unto you," He said. At first the disciples were not sure that it was Jesus. They thought they saw a spirit. They were afraid.

Then Jesus said: "Why are you afraid? Why do you doubt? Look at the marks the nails made in My hands and feet, and see that it is I." Jesus showed His disciples His hands and feet.

While they wondered, Jesus said: "Have you anything to eat?" They gave Him some fish and honey, and Jesus ate it.

Now the disciples knew that this was really their Lord who was crucified and had become alive again. Jesus talked to them for a while, and then He was gone.

When Thomas came, the other disciples said: "We have seen the Lord!" But Thomas would not believe them. He said: "Except I see the marks of the nails in His hands and put my finger into His side, I will not believe that Jesus is alive."

A week later the disciples were together again. This time Thomas was with them. Suddenly Jesus was in the room. "Peace be unto you," He said.

Then Jesus turned to Thomas. "Put your finger into the marks of My hands. Also touch the wound in My side. Do not doubt, Thomas, but believe."

Now Thomas believed that Jesus had risen from the dead and was really alive. He said: "My Lord and my God!" Jesus answered: "Thomas, because you have seen me, you have believed. Blessed are they that have not seen and yet have believed."

Luke 24:36-43; John 20:19-29

"It Is the Lord"

Feed My Lambs

One day Simon Peter and John and five other disciples were together at the Sea of Galilee. "I am going fishing," said Peter. "We will go along," they answered. So they rowed their boat out on the sea and fished all night, but they did not catch anything.

The next morning Jesus stood on the shore, but the disciples did not know it was Jesus. He called to them and asked whether they had caught anything.

They answered, "No." He said to them: "Throw your nets out on the right side of the boat." They obeyed, and soon they were not able to pull up the net because there were so many fish in it.

John knew now who the Man on the shore was. "It is the Lord," he said. When Simon Peter heard that it was the Lord, he put on his coat and jumped into the water to wade to the shore. The other disciples came in the boat, dragging the net with fish.

As soon as they had come to land, they saw a fire there, and fish laid on it, and bread.

Jesus said to them: "Come and dine."

After the disciples had eaten, Jesus said to Simon Peter: "Simon, do you love Me more than these?" Peter answered: "Yes, Lord, You know that I love You." Jesus said to him: "Feed My lambs."

Again Jesus said: "Simon, do you love Me?" Peter answered: "Yes, Lord, You know that I love You." Jesus said: "Feed My sheep."

Then, for the third time, Jesus asked: "Simon, do you love Me?" Now Peter was sad because Jesus had asked him this question the third time. He remembered how he had three times denied Jesus in the house of the high priest. He was truly sorry for that, and therefore he said: "Lord, You know all things; You know that I love You." Jesus said to him: "Feed My sheep."

Jesus had fully forgiven Peter's sin, and Peter was now to teach both the little children and grown people about Jesus the Savior.

John 21:1-19

"All Power Is Given unto Me in Heaven and in Earth"

The Great Commission

Long before His resurrection Jesus had chosen twelve disciples to be His helpers. For about three years they heard His teachings and saw His miracles and helped Him in His work. In this way Jesus trained them for the work which He wanted them to do for Him.

Now Jesus had suffered and died for the sins of all men. On the third day He had risen from the dead. His work on earth was finished, and soon He would return to heaven.

But Jesus remained on earth for forty days after His resurrection. During that time He often appeared to His disciples. He wanted to make them sure that He was risen. He also stayed to tell them more about their work for Him.

One day the disciples and many other followers of Jesus went to Galilee. There they met on a mountain where Jesus had promised to come to them.

When Jesus appeared, they bowed their heads and worshiped Him. Then Jesus came near and began to speak. He said: "All power is given unto Me in heaven and in earth. Go ye, therefore, and teach all nations, baptizing them in the name of the Father and of the Son and of the Holy Ghost."

This was the important work for which Jesus had trained His disciples. They were to go and tell all people about Jesus, their Lord and Savior, and baptize them. We, too, are to go and teach others. All who believe in Jesus and are baptized will be saved and will one day be with Jesus in heaven.

Those who believe in Jesus and are baptized are also to live as His children. That is why Jesus added: "Teach them to observe all things whatsoever I have commanded you." "To observe" means to believe and do.

This command is called the Great Commission. Teaching the Word of God to all nations is the greatest and most important work in the world.

It is not easy work, but Jesus gave a wonderful promise to all who do this work. He said: "Lo, I am with you alway, even unto the end of the world."

Matthew 28:16-20; Mark 16:14-18

The Disciples Looked into Heaven as He Went Up

The Ascension of Jesus

On the fortieth day after Easter the disciples of Jesus were again together in Jerusalem, and Jesus was with them. It was Jesus' last day on earth, and He had many things to say to the disciples. Especially did He speak about the wonderful things that had happened in the past few weeks—things which had been foretold about Him in the Bible.

Jesus helped them understand the Bible. He said to them: "It is written in the Bible that the Savior should suffer and rise from the dead the third day, and that the good news of forgiveness should be told to all people. And you are witnesses of these things."

Then Jesus commanded them not to leave Jerusalem, but to wait for the gift of the Holy Spirit. He said: "You shall receive power after the Holy Ghost has come upon you, and you shall be witnesses for Me in Jerusalem and in all Judea and in Samaria and in all the earth."

Having spoken these words He led them out to Bethany, on the Mount of Olives. There He lifted up His hands and blessed them. While He blessed them, He was taken from them and carried up into heaven.

When the disciples looked toward heaven as He went up, two men suddenly stood by them, clothed in white. They said: "You men of Galilee, why do you stand and look up to heaven? This same Jesus shall come again just as you have seen Him go into heaven."

The disciples now returned to Jerusalem with great joy and were in the Temple most of the time, praising God.

Mark 16:19-20; Luke 24:50-53; Acts 1:3-12

Tongues of Fire on Each of the Disciples

The First Pentecost

Pentecost was a great holy day of the people. It was kept fifty days after the Passover. Many would come together in Jerusalem for this holy day. On this day the disciples were all together in one place.

Suddenly a sound like a rushing mighty wind was heard. The Holy Spirit came to the disciples, and soon one could see little tongues like fire on each one of the disciples as a sign that the Holy Spirit had been sent to them.

Another miracle was that every disciple could speak in languages which he had never learned before. Soon the people began to hear of these wonderful things. They hurried to see the disciples and to hear what they had to say.

Peter now stood up and began to speak to the people. He told them that what was happening was the work of the Holy Spirit. He told them that God had sent His Son, Jesus, to be the Savior of the world, but that they had crucified Him. On the third day, however, He had risen from the dead and was now alive.

Many of the people, when they heard Peter's words, were troubled and afraid because of their sins. They asked the disciples: "What shall we do?"

The disciples said: "Be truly sorry for your sins, and be baptized in the name of Jesus for the forgiveness of sins." More than three thousand people believed in Jesus and received forgiveness of sins on that first Pentecost.

This was the work of the Holy Spirit. Even today He works whenever the story of Jesus, the Savior, is told.

Acts 2:1-41

At Once the Man's Feet and Ankles Became Strong

Healing the Lame Man

In Jerusalem there lived a certain lame man. He was forty years old, and he had never been able to walk. Every day his friends brought him to the temple. There he sat at one of the gates and begged. Often kind people gave him some money.

One afternoon Peter and John went to the Temple to pray. The lame man saw them come. When they were near, he held out his hand and begged for money.

Peter and John stopped, and Peter spoke to the man. He said: "Look at us."

The lame man did as he was told. He thought Peter and John were going to give him some money. But Peter said: "I have no money, but I have something else, and that I will give you. In the name of Jesus Christ, stand up and walk!"

As Peter said this, he took hold of the man's right hand and lifted him up. At once the man's feet and ankles became strong. He stood and walked. He went into the temple, leaping and praising God.

There were many people in the temple. They saw the man leap, and they heard him praise God. They thought, "Why, this is the same man who was lame and who sat at the gate and begged! What happened that he can walk now?"

The people looked at the man. They also looked at Peter and John. Peter said to them: "Why do you look at us as though we made this man walk with *our* power?"

Then Peter spoke to the people about Jesus, the Savior. He said: "You brought Jesus before Pilate. You spoke against Jesus when Pilate wanted to set Him free. You killed Jesus, whom God has raised from the dead. It is Jesus who made this man strong before you all. Be sorry for your sins so that they will be taken away."

Many of the people who heard this were led to believe in Jesus. And the number of people who believed grew to about five thousand.

Acts 3:1-19

Philip and the Ethiopian

The Man of Ethiopia

Soon after Pentecost the believers in Jerusalem were in trouble. They were being arrested and put in jail. They had to go to other places to be safe. But wherever they went, they told the story of Jesus. Philip also left Jerusalem. He was one of the men who helped Peter and the other Apostles in their work. He went to Samaria to preach about Jesus.

One day the angel of the Lord said to him: "Go down along the road that leads from Jerusalem to Gaza." At once Philip obeyed and went. On this road he saw a dark-skinned man riding in a fine chariot.

The man was an officer of the queen of Ethiopia. He had been in Jerusalem and was now going back to his own country. As he rode, he was reading in the Bible what one of the Prophets had written about Jesus.

As Philip came near the chariot, he heard the man reading. "Do you understand what you are reading?" he asked. The man answered: "How can I, unless someone helps me?"

Then he asked Philip to come up and sit with him. Philip sat beside him and explained the words of the Bible. He told the man about Jesus, the Savior, who had died for the sins of all people.

As they were riding along, they came to some water. The Ethiopian said: "Here is water. May I not be baptized?" Philip answered: "Yes, you may be baptized."

The man now stopped the chariot, and they both went down to the water, and Philip baptized him. As soon as this was done, the Holy Spirit took Philip away to another place. But the man went on his way full of joy, for he knew that God had forgiven him all his sins.

Acts 8:1-8, 26-40

His Chains Fell Off, and the Angel Told Peter to
Put on His Coat and Follow Him

Peter's Deliverance from Prison

The Christians in Jerusalem were in great danger, for wicked King Herod began to trouble the church. He killed James, one of the twelve apostles, with the sword. Seeing how much this pleased the enemies of the Christians, he put Peter in prison. This happened just before the day we now call Easter. Herod intended to have Peter put to death after Easter.

The Christians were greatly troubled because Peter too was to be killed. So they met for prayer in the house of Mary, the mother of John. They asked Jesus to save Peter from death.

The night before Peter was to die, a strange thing happened. He was sleeping between two soldiers. He was bound with chains, and soldiers were watching at the door.

An angel touched Peter and woke him up. His chains fell off, and the angel told Peter to put on his coat and follow him. Peter thought he was dreaming. But the angel led him past the soldiers.

When they came to the big iron gate of the prison, it opened by itself. A minute later they were on the street, and the angel left Peter.

Now Peter knew he had not been dreaming. He said, "I am sure the Lord has sent His angel to save me from Herod." He hurried to the home of Mary. He knocked at the door and told who he was.

The girl who came to the door was so excited that she forgot to let him in. She ran to the friends of Peter and cried: "Peter has come." At first they did not believe her. "It must be his spirit," they said.

But Peter kept on knocking, and when they opened the door and saw him, they were very much surprised.

As soon as they were quiet, Peter told them how the Lord had brought him out of prison. The same night he went away to a place where Herod would not find him.

Acts 12:1-17

The People Loved Dorcas Because She Was Kind and Good

Dorcas

Before Jesus rose into heaven, He told His disciples to teach the Word of God in nearby and in faraway places. The disciples went out and taught the people, as Jesus had said.

Wherever they taught, the Holy Spirit led people to believe in Jesus. Soon there were believing people in many cities and towns.

Along the seashore about forty miles from Jerusalem there was a city called Joppa. Some who believed in Jesus lived there, too. One of them was a woman whose name was Dorcas. Dorcas loved the Lord; therefore she was kind and good and felt sorry for anyone who was in trouble.

There were some poor people in Joppa. Dorcas helped them. She sewed and made clothing and gave it to them. The people of Joppa loved Dorcas because she was kind and good.

One day Dorcas became sick, and after a while she died. Some of her friends heard that Peter was in a city nearby, so they sent for Peter.

When Peter came, he went into the room where Dorcas lay. The friends of Dorcas stood around, crying. They showed Peter the coats and other clothes that Dorcas had made for them.

After a little while, Peter asked everyone to leave the room. When they had gone out, Peter knelt down and prayed. Then he looked at Dorcas and said: "Dorcas, arise!"

As soon as Peter had said this, Dorcas opened her eyes. Peter took hold of her hand and helped her stand up. He called her friends into the room, and they were very, very happy to see Dorcas standing there alive.

All the people of Joppa heard about Dorcas —how she had been dead and was made alive again. Many of the people who heard this believed in Jesus. For they knew that Peter had not made Dorcas alive with his own power but with the power of Jesus.

Acts 9:36-42

Saul Said, "Who Are You, Lord?"

The Conversion of Saul

One of the greatest enemies of the Christians was a man whose name was Saul. At one time he went from house to house and arrested the Christians and put them into prison.

One day he went to the high priest in Jerusalem.

He asked for letters which would introduce him to the church leaders in Damascus. He wanted to arrest the Christians in Damascus, too, and bring them bound to Jerusalem.

The high priest gave Saul the letters, and Saul, together with some other men, went to Damascus.

As Saul and his men came to Damascus, suddenly a light from heaven shone around him. Saul and his men fell to the ground.

Then Saul heard a voice saying to him: "Saul, Saul, why are you persecuting Me?" Saul said: "Who are You, Lord?"

The voice answered: "I am Jesus, whom you are persecuting." Saul trembled and said: "Lord, what do You want me to do?" The Lord Jesus answered: "Get up, and go into the city, and you will be told what you must do."

Saul arose from the ground and opened his eyes, but he could not see! The other men had to lead him by the hand.

They brought him to Damascus, to the house of a friend whose name was Judas. There he stayed for three days without being able to see. Nor did he eat or drink anything.

In Damascus there lived a Christian whose name was Ananias. The Lord appeared to him and said: "Arise, and go into the street which is called Straight, and ask at the house of Judas for a man called Saul." Ananias answered: "Lord, I have heard how much evil this man has done to the Christians in Jerusalem. Here he has permission to arrest all who call on Your name."

But the Lord said: "Go, for I have chosen him to be My servant to preach to the Gentiles." So Ananias went.

Ananias found Saul and he laid his hands on him and said: "Brother Saul, the Lord Jesus, who appeared to you on the way, has sent me. He wants you to receive your sight and to be filled with the Holy Spirit."

All at once Saul could see again, and he arose and was baptized. No longer did he want to hurt the Christians, for now he was a Christian himself.

From that time on he used his other name—Paul—and became a great missionary for Jesus. He traveled to many faraway places to tell sinners about Jesus, the Savior.

Acts 8:3; 9:1-22

Timothy

Timothy

In a land far away there lived a boy named Timothy. His mother's name was Eunice, and his grandmother's name was Lois. Timothy lived with his mother and grandmother. They loved God, and Timothy loved Him, too.

Ever since Timothy was a very little boy, his mother and his grandmother taught him the Word of God. Timothy loved the Word of God, and he never forgot what he learned.

One day, when Timothy was still young, a missionary of Jesus came to the city where he lived. This missionary was Paul.

He taught the people, saying: "Jesus is the Son of God and the Savior from sin." Timothy and his mother and grandmother heard Paul, and they believed in Jesus as the promised Savior.

Later Paul came back to the same place. The Christians told Paul that Timothy was a fine Christian and studied God's Word.

Paul was so pleased that he asked Timothy to come with him. He wanted Timothy to help him teach people in other places about Jesus the Savior.

Timothy prayed to the Lord and then decided to go. He believed that this was what God wanted him to do.

So Timothy went away with Paul, and everywhere he went he told boys and girls, fathers and mothers, grandfathers and grandmothers Bible stories about Jesus, so that they, too, might believe in Him and be saved.

Acts 16:1-5; 1 and 2 Timothy

Children Who Sang in the Temple

(See page 137)